EGYPTIAN PLACES

EGYPTIAN PLACES

An Illustrated Travelogue

HENRY DAVID AYON

ORO EDITIONS
NOVATO, CALIFORNIA

To Paula

My lifelong traveling companion

Trajan's Kiosk / Philae Island

CONTENTS

Foreword

TEMPLE OF DENDUR

AS A RECENT GRADUATE employed at the office of Roche Dinkeloo Architects in the mid 1970s, I was part of a team building a model of the Temple of Dendur (completed 10 BC), a gift from Egypt to the United States for its assistance in saving various sites threatened by the construction of the Aswan High Dam. The temple and a freestanding stone entry gate were to be reassembled and featured in a new wing of the Metropolitan Museum of Art in New York City, as part of its Egyptian Collection. This relatively minor structure, exquisite in detail and scale, was my first direct contact with the wonders of ancient Egyptian architecture.

Although small, this temple is laid out with many of the same pieces, in miniature, as the massive temples I was to visit decades later:

- Entry Gate (Pylon) with Cavetto Fascia
- Courtyard
- Pronaos (Vestibule)
- Antechamber
- Sanctuary
- Battered Walls
- Ashlar Stone Blocks

This was an unusual assignment to be working on in the office of a well-known modern architect near the end of the 20th century. I never expected to make contact with an artifact so ancient and so exotic in the context of our work environment. Everything about this ancient edifice was, for me, new: the antiquity of the structure, the exotic iconography, and, stylistically, the non-Classical (Greek or Roman) ornament.

Once installed, the remarkable physical presence of battered walls, entry portal, hieroglyphic display, and the subtle tension of the spatial "cube" between portal and temple were inspiring and moving.

Decades later, on an excursion that would take us from congested present-day Cairo to the majestic temples along the Nile and then on to remote Abu Simbel, my point of reference was always the tiny Temple of Dendur: its stones were the stones we would encounter at Karnak and Edfu, its hieroglyphics were the same images we would see displayed on numerous sacred buildings, and its mysteries drew their inspiration from the same ancient land in the Sahara Desert of North Africa.

This volume is a combination of illustrations (colored drawings and sepia variations), factual information, and architectural commentary regarding the twelve Egyptian sacred sites we visited on our journey to temples and pyramids along the Nile.

Temple of Dendur: Metropolitan Museum / New York

Art + Architecture: I

FOR THE VAST MAJORITY OF US, exposure to the culture and wonders of ancient Egypt comes by way of popular media: the "curse of the mummy" (dead, yet, unfortunately, not quite dead), the Giza Pyramid (massive), and hissing cobras (resist the temptation to open any small basket). Their culture appeared to be mysterious, larger than life, and dangerous, and the present-day political climate seems to hold its own ambiguities and potential jeopardy. Yet such was the allure that we made the journey, with the hope for making it back architecturally inspired and culturally enlightened.

So we went: At the end of our fourteen-hour flight, the view on our descent into Cairo International Airport gave us a panorama of what appeared to be a planet of sand, just sand, and an emerald strip snaking north/south with small verdant oases of green scattered around the landscape. After deplaning, the remarkable differences in our cultures started with a line of men kneeling in prayer near the baggage carousel and ended with the purchase of a plastic scarab souvenir, just before our return flight.

To create works of such refinement and sophistication, as we experienced in our travels there, required an advanced civilization whose prosperity and social stability allowed it to move beyond the needs of every-day survival into the power and delight of artistic expression. By visiting mosques, temples, churches, and pyramids, we came closer to understanding the creative intersections of cultures and religions, but no closer to solving any of the seemingly unsolvable enigmas of ancient or contemporary Egypt.

FACTS + OPINIONS: In ancient Egypt, death and the afterlife were the obsessions of a culture ruled by a pharaoh who was also a deity figure and guided by a host of influential temple priests who dealt in the occult. Their religious dogma was a faith-based ideology deriving its beliefs from observable, natural phenomena, and human destiny was played out in relation to a supernaturally defined universal cosmic order. This faith was given physical shape and meaning through iconography and ritual, and the architecture, placed in open, featureless landscapes of rock and sand along the green alluvial band of the Nile, exhibited the fundamental signs and symbols of this theology to a largely illiterate population.

While the mythographers created the various gods, defined their natures, and established their domains in numerous texts and mystical dramas that formed the substance of their history and faith, the artist brought them to life with pictorial references conspicuously engraved on every public building.

In this myth-centered, death-obsessed culture, an Egyptian's final destiny was a combination of two factors: In life, it was a person's conduct in the face of indeterminable fate; in death, it was determinable fate based on personal conduct in life. The so-called "weighing of the heart," a ritual presided over by Osiris and Thoth in the Duat, the realm of the dead, placed an individual's life conduct (as represented by the heart) against a feather (representing truth) on opposite trays of a scale. Balance meant the individual was granted eternal life. If the heart was heavier, indicating a life of sin, it would be immediately devoured by Ammit, "the soul-eater," a demon with the head of a crocodile, the torso of a lion, and the lower body of a hippopotamus, an unattractive consequence from almost any perspective.

Egypt's rampant iconography and extravagant ornament represents (either literal or imagined) inherited associations from nature, both conscious and subconscious (what Jung might have referred to as "primordial images"). The artist (priest) incorporated cultural aspirations into an art and architecture that had numerous associations with Egyptian life, works that perfectly responded to the color and terrain of the Sahara and the Nile. The natural elements of earth, fire, water, and air took on built form in the abstractions of the triangle, the circle, the line, and the arc.

Triangle: In the archetypal pyramid we have a simulation of the mountain form—mammoth, dense and sheltering. It rises majestically above the desert plateau, a stunning presence as powerful as any formation created by nature.

Circle: The giver of life is Amun-Ra, the great sun god, symbolically represented by the massive solar disc. He is reborn each day as he rises in the east and dies each night as he descends below the western horizon.

Line: The sustainer of life is the Nile, its waters represent rejuvenation and constitute the domain of Sobek, the crocodile-headed god.

Arc: The goddess Nut, the embodiment of the heavens, is depicted as a star-spangled and inverted elongated U-shape, her arms and legs angled down with her torso curving to form the sky vault, spanning from sundown to sunrise.

So every Egyptian, both pharaoh and common man, spent each day among the gods, protected and aided by their presence in the various forms of nature. Each individual held their belief as sacred, and in belief there arose a trust in the power of the ancient deities to sustain the cosmic balance (Ma'at) and the immutable integrity of eternal life.

Over the next two weeks, we walked among the old gods, surrounded by the bird-headed, the cow-eared, and the jackal-faced among the image-rich structures here. With the force of their gods so stunningly displayed, we ultimately wondered: Where do the souls of the ancients now reside? Are they alive in the afterlife or are they lost for all time? By the end of our journey we concluded that if one knew the answers to these and other mysteries, it would not lessen the bewitching magnetism of the cultural remains or the strange enchantment of their divine and bizarre magical beings.

Hieroglyph: Cartouche of Ramesses II

EGYPTIAN PLACES

Introduction: PRIMAL IMAGININGS

> *The essential qualities of Egyptian works are prodigious solidity and wonderful magnitude. These are the leading objects and prominent features in their architecture and sculpture. Indeed, in all their works everything seems calculated for eternity; and if solidity, quantity, mass, and breadth of light and shadow were the only requisites in architecture, we should find all that could be desired in the works of the Egyptians.*
>
> —Sir John Soane, Royal Academy Lectures I, 1819

Silence + Eternity / Time

A PALPABLE, AT TIMES SPELLBINDING, aura of both pervasive and profound mystery surrounds the desert culture of ancient Egypt, its various ritualistic practices, and its curious polytheism. We sensed this singular ambiance in the silent remains of each site visited on our journey. All Egyptian ruins are adorned with the hermetic notations of this antique civilization whose obsession was conjuring the magical means of extending life and establishing a path to eternity. This aura is a phantom presence that can be felt when stepping into the myth-centered ethos that occupies a dark temple chamber, bisected by a single sliver of sunlight, such as we gazed upon in the temple at Dendera, or sensed in the arcane carvings of deities and supernatural encounters animating the walls of a narrow, subterranean crypt, once sealed for millennia. The vacant temples and pyramids that once beheld a ritualized conjuring of occult forces, the air resounding with prayers amid sacrificial burnings to their gods, are now mute—the silence sharpened and the enigmas further deepened by the obfuscation of distant, lost time.

Travelers journey to Egypt to be awed and even overwhelmed by the richness and scale of the ancient constructions. To enter that world, it is necessary to welcome a certain amount of credulity (as I have done in my comments) about the divinity of the pharaohs and the existence of Egyptian gods. True or not, these pagan beliefs inspired the entire culture and guided its efforts into the various artistic manifestations that have shaped its remarkable legacy.

For us, the remains of ancient dynasties proved to be the means and the media of our time travel, a complex shifting in multiple directions through the accreted layers of 4,500 years of history and art in a land of infinite contrasts: In the center of a 21st-century metropolis, we studied the blackened flesh of mummies cocooned in sepia-stained wrappings, thousands of years old, now enshrined in a climate-controlled gallery; then, air-conditioned transport carried us to the edge of the Sahara desert to photograph the Pharaoh Khufu's wooden "solar boat" now suspended in a futuristic, multifaceted metal and glass pavilion adjacent to the Great Giza Pyramid.

In every artifact or ruin, from diminutive, cultic figurines to the mammoth sculptures of Ramesses II at Abu Simbel, we experienced a unique, personal engagement that created an emotional connection to a particular point in time, an association that was artistic, historic, and cultural, all at once. Who would not respond to the endearing naiveté of two painted eyes on the side of General Sepi's 12th-century wooden coffin, positioned to allow him to look east to the rising sun and the birth of the god Amun-Ra from the afterlife? And who would not be moved by the poignancy in the benign smile of King Tut-ankh-amun's burial mask (the Egyptians had presumably conquered death, after all), or the four sculpted winged goddesses at his golden sarcophagus, arms outstretched to embrace and protect the king for all time? In each discovery, as interpreted by our collective conscience and our individual experience, a resonant vibration echoes upward from remote, distant time, through silence, into the light of the present where our own imaginings again bring it to life.

Ancient Egypt's remarkable oddities and monuments have inspired and sustained a centuries-old, universal fascination with the land and history of the pharaohs that shows no sign, either in scholarly research or in popular culture, of abating. We were drawn to Egypt by the mythic attraction and opulent exoticism of the land of the pharaohs, its evocative structures and splendid iconography as represented by the Giza pyramids and Sphinx, the flooded Nile cutting through the Sahara Desert, bizarre symbology and pictographs, and a wild phantasmagoria of imagined (at least as far as we know), animal-headed, human-bodied deities

Seven Doors: Temple of Osiris Hek-Djet / Karnak

who protected and ensured the fundamental stability of the cosmos against chaos (represented by the deities Ma'at and Apophis, respectively), on behalf of mankind.

What gave rise to these ancient gods? Pharaonic Egypt's limited knowledge of the mechanics controlling the universe surely posed significant questions: Why did the Nile flood? Who or what destroyed a season's crops? And, most importantly, what happened to an individual's soul (ba) after death? A divination of the visible, natural world by the elect deduced, with a reasoned belief, the existence of a supernatural, parallel macrocosm of earth gods and their respective realms, deities that resisted or promoted the forces of chaos and influenced the outcome of universal fate in exchange for being honored daily in cultic ceremony conducted by temple priests. This cosmic balance and the individual's transition into the afterlife became a persistent fixation, addressed in complex rituals defined by prayers and offerings.

As a physical representation, their gods were imagined to be more than human in appearance: They assumed, in part, the physical, zoomorphic characteristics of the animal life about them, in what might be considered a relevant and consistent congruence with nature. The appearance and physical traits characterizing this myriad of gods reflected the particular qualities of the associated animal: in Sobek, the ferocity of the crocodile; in Hathor, motherhood, benign and nurturing. As an indication of the many concerns affecting the daily life of man and pharaoh, the list of Egyptian gods populating earth, river, and sky are numerous and their attributes varied. To us these fanciful animal-headed figures in Egyptian mythology appear nonsensical (as they did to the Romans and the Greeks), but there was logic in their divining, and, ultimately, belief in their existence and faith in the power of their influence. Despite periods of Christianity and the dominance of Islam, the old gods here, seemingly everywhere from temple to souvenir, will always typify this ancient culture and the incarnate, supernatural mysteries of Egypt.

Aesthetics

"IS IT ART?" This complex question, which has been hotly debated for centuries, and ramified into many aspects of daily life, must be re-interpreted by each new generation. In the last century, Anthony Burgess defined art as: "the disposition of natural material to a formal end which shall enlighten the imagination," (Burgess 1986, 100) an observation one could call brilliant in its brevity and weight, rightly acknowledging the role of nature in its equation, yet pliant enough to accommodate new aesthetic expressions.

We may consider a sound measure of great art to be the assessment by credible critics and connoisseurs who hold a work in high esteem over eras of changing tastes; if a society's art is the mirror of its culture, the works of ancient Egypt are as remarkable as any world civilization and have certainly stood the test of time in terms of quality of execution and artistic merit. In art, once past utility, there is a progression to ornament and refinement, and we see this elevation in nearly every aspect of mature Egyptian high art. After 3,000 years, it still has the power to impress the scholar and astound the traveler.

ALL GREAT ART and architecture aspire to nature in its fundamental properties of structure, pattern, and material. It is a studied response to the world of natural order and natural beauty, either in harmony or in contrast. An Art Nouveau interior, for example, creates a floating, floriated environment of sinuous tendrils and shimmering surfaces in a nature-based approach to style; in antiquity the Greeks introduced foliage motifs and painted decoration into their art and civic buildings.

In a similar vein, the Egyptians fashioned an aesthetic of building design and ornament creatively patterned on flora and fauna from their immediate, natural surroundings. This striving for a

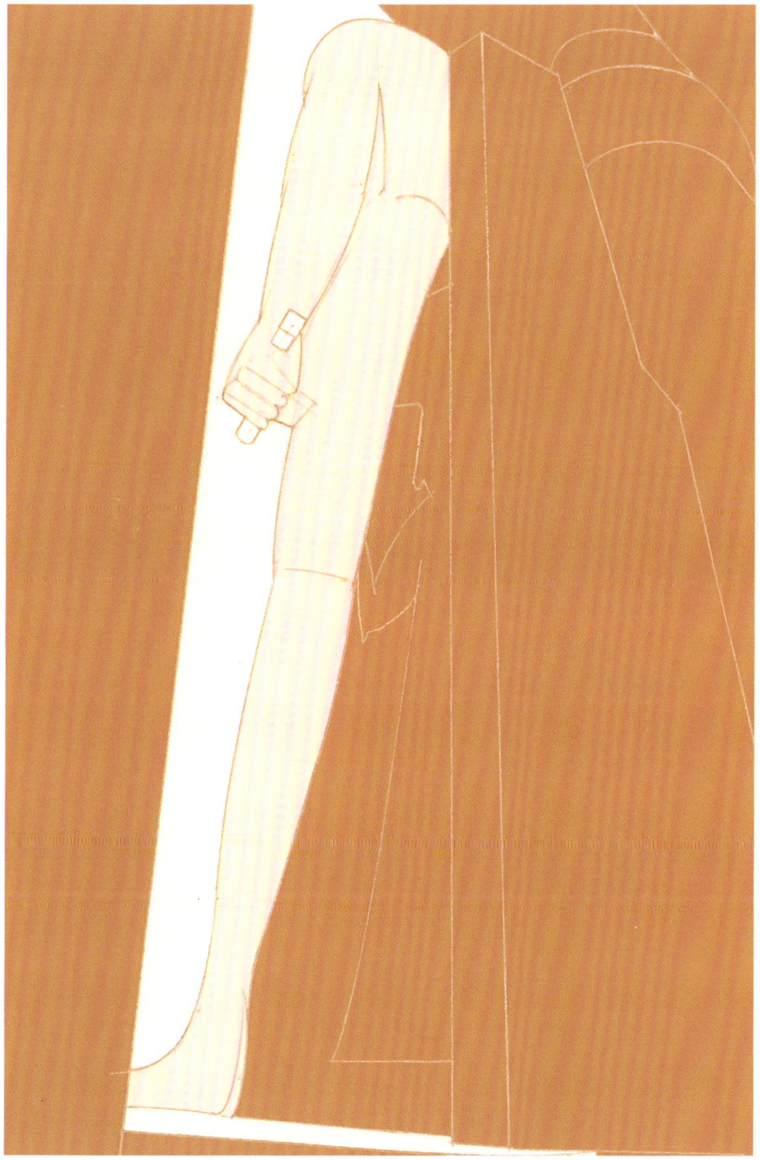

Ramesses II Statue / Luxor

meaningful reference to the greater outside world drew its genius from the teeming environment of the Nile, desert wildlife, and natural phenomena, such as the seemingly omnipotent heat and light of the sun god Amun-Ra or, inversely, the dark, ominous mysteries of night, embodied in the star-studded heaven of the goddess Nut.

Standing amid the ruins of Karnak, one realizes the architecture here could not have been created in any other place than Egypt with its unique artistic response to the land, the desert, and the river. The color, the texture, and the scale are unlike anything in any primitive or modern setting.

This architecture, filled with these references to nature is, even in its most advanced forms, still primal in the weight of its effects as characterized by immense, windowless expanses of wall in simple geometric shapes. Ornament tends to be phantasmal, referring to indigenous flora, and sometimes enlarged to an extraordinary scale and complexity, such as the engaged columns at Philae's mammisi structure whose capitals "blossom" into huge, voluptuous leafage, springing from vertical, reed-like banding. The expression, however, may be a super-sized abstraction, such as the pyramidal form as "mountain," compellingly introduced in the primordial angularity of Saqqara's Step Pyramid.

In the temples, especially, building surfaces became the media for depicting pharaoh–deity engagement, rituals, and civic propaganda, mixing art with communication. Texts were carved into stone as an eternal witness to the modes and rituals of their culture, and figural depiction of gods and pharaohs were cut deep into a flat rock plane, shaped in a way that brilliantly conveyed the sense of a three-dimensional body, the style intending to "vitalize the magic power of the animated world of images" (Arnold 1999, 28).

Thus, a reasoned symbiosis of man and nature was fantasized into myth, acted out in supernatural tales, and conspicuously displayed in an architecture constructed to stand for eternity.

In its human manifestation, the pharaoh wore the pschent, the headdress of the double crown, representing the unification of the two lands—Upper and Lower Egypt—acknowledging his symbolic embodiment of two regions merged into one nation, as nature subsumed by man.

These splendid and seductive curiosities of men and gods that inhabit the history and myths of ancient Egypt, as chronicled in their hieroglyphics and carvings, are ubiquitous among the relics (too ubiquitous, many would say) but most visibly displayed in the preternatural illustrations and texts covering Egyptian architecture.

Two significant building types accommodated the supplications of man to god and man to eternity in Egypt's efforts to influence the outcome of fate: the temple (where priestly daily rituals sustained the cosmic order or Ma'at) and the tomb (a reliquary for articles needed in the next life and a home for the mummified body, where a spiritually tethered soul would return periodically). In both, the sequestered idol or pharaoh dwelt in an exalted dimension of magic and transcendence. On a cosmic scale, each was a crucible for the struggles of personal or universal destiny and each is among the greatest wonders of antiquity, stunning monuments to the unknown and the unknowable, testaments to both faith and hope, rich with the intricacies of pervasive iconography and intimate human ceremony, yet massive enough to contain the soul of an ancient god.

Exterior Passage between Pylons above a Temple Entry Gate

The Egyptian Temple

IT IS DIFFICULT TO NOT be impressed by the pyramids, especially Khufu's great tomb at Giza, its formidable mass tapering upward from a width of 755 feet at its base to zero at its peak, hundreds of feet in the air: impressive and overwhelming. But for many, Egyptian temples hold more interest and fascination in the greater variety of their building forms, space shaping, and detail. (With the true polyhedral pyramids, the inherent sterility of their perfection—four flawless triangular faces meeting at an immeasurable intersection, the structure free of iconography and surface modulation—offers a more rational, less complex visual experience.)

All of the great world religions created worship spaces meant to accommodate large congregations of the devout in rooms designed to inspire and uplift the spirit through the beauty of architecture and commonality of fellowship. Not so with the temples here: Each was a massive, windowless block of dense construction and dark spaces, visited by temple priests and few others—once a hermetic compound of dense mysteries and arcane ritual, now vacant of life or gods.

Temple of Amun / Karnak

Luxor Temple / Luxor

Temple of Horus: Entrance Panorama / Edfu

THE TEMPLES ALONG THE NILE offer the traveler a rich and, at times, profound experience with their overlapping of cultures, magnificent art and architecture, mythic dramaturgy, and political intrigue—a captivating historical panorama that swings from 3,000 BC to the present. So these worship complexes are understandably the most visited sites from ancient Egypt (Karnak and Luxor have often been described as the "world's greatest open-air museum") after the wonders of Giza.

Egypt's pharaohs, as a display of prosperity and strength, expended significant resources on temple and necropolis. Modest domestic or local shrines developed into huge temple districts of worship and administration. From a polytheistic constellation of deities, one god or a variant of merged gods was chosen to preside over a particular region (somewhat like a patron saint), and eventually, all forty-two nomes or states of Egypt had their own deity/protector and the number of temples proliferated over time.

In the often stately temples of ancient Greece, the cult effigy also resided in a mystical, darkened space of a windowless interior "cella," but the edifice itself is sited with a sensitivity to variations in elevation between mountain and ocean and often oriented to align with spectacular Aegean vistas (the French-Swiss architect Le Corbusier writes movingly of this response to landscape in his 1923 volume *Vers une Architecture*) (Le Corbusier 1931, 173).

In contrast, Egyptian temple precincts were encircled by high masonry walls and the orientation is inward, fully concentrated on the cult figure sheltered within the deity chamber. Once we entered the walls of the temple complex, there were no views to the outside world as we moved through entry gate, inner courts, pronaoi (vestibules), hypostyle halls, and auxiliary chambers, finally arriving at the sanctuary, the dwelling place of the deity.

Functionally, auxiliary spaces within the temple structure included small shrine chambers, stairs (to the roof), crypts, and storerooms—all necessary to support the requirements of ritual and administration. An array of related temple complex structures may have included a mammisi ("birth house," a small chapel used for cultic ceremony), obelisks, a man-made sacred lake, living quarters for the priests, supplemental storage, and work facilities.

Stylistic features of the architecture included massive, opaque building volumes of solid stone, ornate column capitals (flora inspired or deity-headed, for example), battered pylons, temple building enclosure walls (concentric with the worship space), hieroglyphic texts, pictographs, and cavetto moldings. All the major figures depicted on façades—gods, goddesses, pharaohs, and animals, as well as architectural ornament, would have been rendered in vivid colors on a canvas of stone, once brilliantly lit by the Saharan sun. A few of the ruin sites still retain areas of faded paint, allowing us to imagine mythic figures and decoration animated by a riot of color that would have been bewildering in its effect.

The temple interior, however, with its various windowless chambers, created a mystical place of dimly lit, evocative, unfolding space, leading ultimately to the "sanctum sanctorum" of the deity. As the spiritual center and power source of the temple precinct, the cult idol resided in the exalted solitude of its chamber, physically protected by layers of massive stone walls and surrounded by hundreds of mythic characters, apotropaic figures, and magic spells: daunting, but I would agree with Cyril Connolly that one might raise a bemused eyebrow when considering the cultic rituals of their most devout ceremonies: "an Egyptian temple: magnificent to look at and inside, a priest singing a hymn to a cat or a crocodile" (Connolly 1984, 70). Such were their beliefs.

Each day, the temple priests, to ensure the continuity of cosmic balance, performed rituals of idol worship and ceremonies of propitiation that included icon bathing, makeup-application (the raising of the other eyebrow), and changing of clothing and jewelry on the cult effigy. The pharaoh, despite his direct relationship to the gods, was rarely, if ever, present at the ceremonies, and, because the temple was not a place of public worship, the general population was not allowed to view or assist in the rituals, thus intensifying the atmosphere of profound mystery surrounding the modes and nature of their practices. As temple residents and daily administrators to the various idols, the priests eventually assumed great wealth and wielded great influence over Egyptian culture.

Building structure set its own impositions on the elements with size (invariably large) and material (stone, heavy) constraints. Structural beams of stone were difficult to fabricate and place and required massive stone columns to carry the weight, which also limited the span from column to column. The Egyptians, however, battered pylons to lessen the apparent mass, tapered tall stone columns, gracefully introduced floral references at column capitals and used paint to differentiate the components and enliven stone surfaces, all to impressive visual effect. However, by the twilight of pharaonic rule, temple design had been systematized into an architectural template of building pieces arranged in a specific relationship within the worship compound, a practice that discouraged creativity as future designs repeated the same elements and decorative motifs. Exterior ceremonial spaces were designed on a grand scale to accommodate large crowds on festival days when the populace was able to view the idol barque (carried shrine) but not the curtained idol as it was transported to other sites, such as the Amun effigy traveling from Karnak to Luxor. The crowded landscape in and around a temple would have been a dramatic scene of state-sanctioned revelry, composed of throngs of people, processional cavalcades, mythic reenactments in and around the sacred lake, and flying banners—visually, one imagines, not unlike a scene from a 1960s Hollywood biblical blockbuster, just smaller.

Hieroglyph: Horus Lion

Hatshepsut Pier Statue / Mortuary Temple of Hatshepsut

Organizational Layout

FOR THE MOST PART, the temples were nearly symmetrical structures and movement to and from the sanctuary itself was strictly organized along a secure, axial path, emphasizing balance and equilibrium. A procession to the Nile moved through these spaces:

Sanctuary: (fire-lit, dark) The "sanctum sanctorum" or dwelling place of the cult idol effigy positioned near the center of the temple building. The procession departs from the sanctuary, with the idol positioned on the ritual barque, a portable boat-shaped structure.

Hypostyle Hall: (shadowed, half-light, darkened) From the sanctuary, the procession moves through a grid of massive, image-covered columns dimly lit by small clerestory windows above and fire lamps below.

Kiosk: (shaded sunlight) The barque exits the hall and stops in the kiosk, a fabric-roofed, open structure of low intercolumnar walls and expressed columns that serves as a secure place for the cult figure when journeying to other temples. (Trajan's Kiosk at Philae is the best-preserved example of this building type extant in Egypt.)

Temple Forecourt: (full sunlight) The barque moves from the kiosk through a large open public space to the entry gate.

Entry Gate: (shadow) The barque transitions to the outside world as it moves through the entry gate. This portal, contiguous with the flanking pylons of the temple façade, is often adorned with the winged solar disc and capped with a cavetto molding.

Nile Transport: (brilliant, reflected sunlight) The barque is placed on an actual boat to begin its river journey, symbolically merging with the Nile.

Additional terms associated with the temple complex are as follows:

Mammisi: The sacred "birth house," a one-story structure normally positioned in front of the temple and oriented at a right angle to the processional axis centered on the sanctuary. It consisted of interior chambers for rituals and reenactments of myths, including birth myths of the gods. The exterior is distinctive with its three-sided colonnade around the perimeter and intercolumnar screen walls.

Obelisk: A four-sided, tapered figure of stone topped with a pyramidion capstone and adorned with carved hieroglyphics. Pairs often flank the entrance to a temple.

Pylon: Greek for "large entrance gateway." Massive, battered structures flanking the entry gate, up to ten stories in height, displaying carved images of royalty and deities.

Sacred Lake: A man-made body of water adjacent to the temple used by priests for ablution and for enacting mythic narratives.

Sphinx Allée: A continuous line of closely spaced ram-headed sphinxes, flanking the path approach to the entrance of a temple complex.

Temple Enclosing Wall: An unroofed, freestanding stone wall, concentric with the temple worship block. This area provided an additional layer of protection between the sanctuary and the forces of imagined chaos.

Temple Precinct Wall: A high masonry wall of mud brick surrounding the entire temple complex. The brick was normally laid in undulating, curving courses as a metaphor for the Sea of Chaos before the creation of the world.

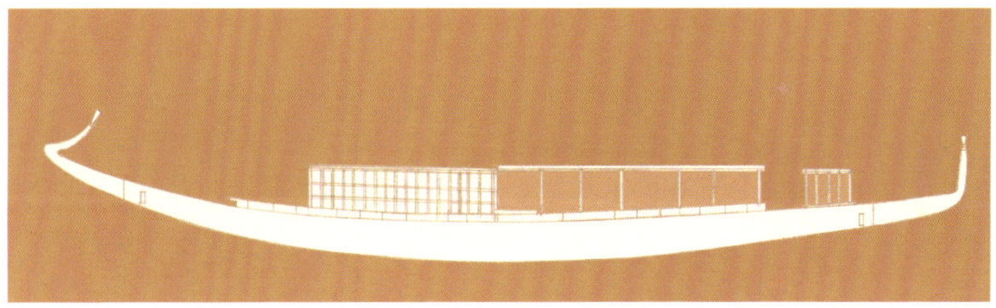

Solar Boat / Giza

Nile View / Philae Island

Temple of Amun: Barbary Lion / Karnak

Ramesses II / Abu Simbel

The Egyptian Pyramid / Tomb

MY FIRST VIEW OF AN EGYPTIAN PYRAMID was from our hotel room in Cairo shortly after arrival. Looking west from our balcony, the tiny, barely discernible triangular shape of Khufu's tomb at Giza, six miles away, was silhouetted against the setting sun, like a giant scarab following Amun-Ra into a blazing sunset. This was hardly the longed-for introduction to the last standing example of the Seven Wonders of the Ancient World that I had envisioned in my late-night, transatlantic thoughts: That would come later.

Then, as the dream sequence of our travels was ending, I saw the same pyramid in the late afternoon from our final hotel on the day of departure. The darkened body of Khufu's massive tomb, now only 400 feet to the west, cast its shadow over the entire courtyard as we craned our necks to take in the massive breadth of its forty-story tall silhouette, and it seemed fitting to be so close to this icon at the dying of the day with the hope of rebirth at the next sunrise, when we would be soon be hundreds of miles away, racing against Amun-Ra's westerly path.

THE PLANNING OF A PHARAOH'S TOMB began at his ascension to the throne, and, considering the magnitude of the undertaking, some were not finished when a king died. Pharaoh Khufu, for example, did survive the twenty years of construction to see his completed Great Pyramid, but King Tut-ankh-amun died suddenly at age nineteen and his entombment in the Valley of the Kings was a hasty undertaking in subterranean chambers perhaps meant for someone else to occupy.

Step Pyramid / Saqqara

Bent Pyramid / Dahshur

Black Pyramid / Dahshur

The Pyramid

A PYRAMID IS, fundamentally, a massive tomb, the final resting place of the pharaoh—a dwelling for his mummified body and a storehouse of essential objects required in the next life, including food, statuary, and even chariots. Here again, the Egyptians worked at a mammoth scale and in perfect, abstract geometry for the shape. Because it was not the scene of public ritual, the sloping, ashlar stone façades were completely smooth and free of carvings or painted images. At its most advanced state, each of the four faces is a pure triangle, with the façades meeting at the apex, the point dissolving into space where, as Scully has observed, "the avoidance of the appearance of weight is almost entirely achieved" (Scully 1991, 27). There are no overt religious pictographs or symbols here, only majesty and the display of pharaonic power, wealth, and extraordinary engineering abilities.

Egypt's pyramids were built to exist for all time with the concept starting in nascent form at Saqqara, achieving the first true pyramid (Red Pyramid) at Dahshur, progressing through the Great Pyramid at Giza, and ending in the 3rd millennium BC with the pyramid of Pepi II. The Great Pyramid, the only surviving structure of the seven wonders of antiquity, remained the tallest structure in the world for thousands of years, until it was surpassed by the Eiffel Tower in 1889. Temples and pyramids created a new aesthetic and a new model for civic architecture—solid, immense, and tall, dominating the desert landscape, calculated to inspire awe and faith in the transformative powers of the ancient gods with the promise of eternity girdled within its sloping walls.

Additional structures related to the pyramid building type:

Causeway: An enclosed stone walled corridor, top lit and narrow in width, linking the valley temple (at the debarking place) and the pyramid mortuary temple (at the foot of the pyramid).

Mortuary Temple: A one-story edifice contiguous with the pyramid, used for the commemoration of the pharaoh's rule and as a location for cult offerings.

Valley Temple: A structure located adjacent to the Nile for the reception of the royal mummified body of the king and a stopping place for a pharaoh's corpse in transit to burial in the pyramid.

The Royal Subterranean Tomb

EGYPT'S MASSIVE, seemingly impregnable pyramids (the pharaoh lying in the center, like a seed in an apple), despite being radiant with spells and charged with the "curse of the mummy" to discourage and bring revenge upon looters, were all eventually robbed of their inestimable riches. In an attempt to thwart thievery and preserve tombs as inviolable, the pharaohs (but also royalty and the wealthy) discontinued the building of pyramid tombs. Instead, subterranean, multiroom rock-cut burial chambers were excavated in the so-called Valley of the Kings, directly across the river from ancient Thebes (Karnak), a practice which lasted for over 500 years.

Since the tombs were intended to be hidden, only the interior chamber walls and corridors were decorated, but that decoration was lavish and detailed. There was often a profusion of intense color (surprisingly vivid today) and legions of characters, both divine and human, portrayed in actions addressing various themes of the afterlife.

Kiosk of Nectanebo / Philae Island

Pyramids / Giza

Pyramids / Giza

Festival Hall of King Tuthmosis III / Karnak

The Architect

ARCHITECTURE MANIFESTS ITSELF in the inspired act of its creation. This act is the practice of making art by an ingenious disposition of natural material, the use of daylight, the manipulation of structure, and the making of space in such a way as to "enlighten the mind" and quicken the pulse, characteristics that may be personal and universal at the same time. Once it is complete, the structure stands as a part of an artistic canon that belongs to the culture that inspired it.

For every architect who walks among these ruins or stands before a temple façade today, there is the discernible, ghostly image of one who came before you, fashioned these works out of raw material quarried from the Saharan plateau thousands of years ago, and then slowly vanished into the formless cloud that is the past, the realm of lost time. With the temple and the tomb, two building types with religious and cosmic purpose, the creators of these monuments became the conduit channeling the cultural elements of "fantasy" and "magic" into a built form that created vast and monumental settings as the residence of an all-puissant, ancient god force.

The stylistic and religious characteristics defining this ethos evolved over hundreds of years and then expired when a new faith arose from the east, one that displaced the old deities who then found asylum in the two-dimensional pictographs and three-dimensional statuary of their sacred architecture.

WHILE A NUMBER of architectural drawings have survived from Egyptian antiquity as papyrus fragments, there is little information about the individual creators of these wonders of the ancient world. This may appear surprising when considering their impressive engineering and the high level of artistic skill evident in the ornament, but we must remember that the major structures took hundreds of years to complete over a number of dynasties, and names and dates may have been swept away in time or just not noted. In addition, the title of "architect," as currently understood, is a fairly recent professional designation, and in ancient Egypt the terms used may have been, variously, "royal master builder," "overseer of construction," or "chief royal master builder," suggesting more emphasis on utility rather than rarefied art.

The vast majority of the builders of tombs and temples, like the creators of the European medieval cathedrals, appeared to have labored in anonymity, their efforts dedicated to god or king; however, two names have emerged as ancient makers of monuments: Imhotep and Senenmut.

Imhotep ("the one who comes in peace" c. 2650 BC): The creator of the brilliant Step Pyramid at Saqqara held the title of "the Chancellor of the King of Lower Egypt, Administrator of the Great Mansion, Hereditary Nobel, Heliopolitan High Priest, Imhotep." He impresses us today as a multitalented polymath and was, to paraphrase an historian regarding another highly gifted figure, indeed more "poly" than anyone of his age. Imhotep was eventually elevated to the position of deity (a status rarely bestowed on present-day architects by their clients) and honored with his own temple on the island of Philae. He transformed the one-story tomb at Saqqara into the Step Pyramid and created a new, magnificent language in the design of royal tombs that would evolve and culminate in the ancient wonders at Giza.

Senenmut ("mother's brother" c. 1460 BC): Queen Hatshepsut's Mortuary Temple at Deir el-Bahri, on the west bank of the Nile, adjacent to the Valley of the Kings, is considered to be the efforts of another polymathic administrator, Senenmut.

He enjoyed an especially close association with the queen, and his titles included, "architect of all the works of the Queen, Chief Guardian of the King's Daughter, Governor of the Royal Palace, Superintendent of the Private Apartments." In addition, Senenmut was in charge of the secular activity at Karnak and carried the title of "great steward of Amun," the dedicatee of the temple.

A thousand years after Khufu's Great Pyramid, his design for Hatshepsut's Mortuary Temple (if it is his work) is a magnificent and unique creation consisting of a series of stepped terraces, connected by wide ramps, set, in contrast, against the backdrop of a rugged mountain range.

The old gods of Egypt ruled here until approximately 400 AD and then were gradually supplanted by Christianity and, subsequently, Islam—the dominant religion and cultural force of modern-day Egypt. Still, the magnificent architecture and the rich panoply of deities that defined Egyptians' ancient beliefs would eventually assume a permanence in world history and art, thus bestowing a kind of immortality to Egypt's gods and people, their once dominant cultural fixation fulfilled.

Today

WE FOUND EGYPT, with its 21st-century technology overlapping the ancient, to remain a land of extreme contrasts: river and desert, superstition and science, reason and instinct, life into death/death into life.

The examples are numerous:

- In the shadow of a monumental temple, among the greatest artistic achievements of the ancient world, stands a kiosk bursting with Barbie-like Isis dolls, pyramid paper weights, plastic scarabs, and other tacky, mythical bric-à-brac. Most of us succumbed to the urge to possess an exotic Egyptian faux fragment, some purchased to adorn our home or person, heroically bargained for (we foolishly believed) in a moment of weakness.

- A thin layer of modernity and prosperity floats above a stratum of national poverty that is both broad and deep. Within Cairo, luxury may be contiguous with abject need. Outside the city limits, there is a world still ancient in pace, culture, and technology, accessed by dirt roads or dusty streets, where the populace live as their ancestors lived, with only a modicum of change.

- The ancient practice of the Muslim summons to worship five times a day is now mechanically amplified through speakers mounted on minarets, and the prayers stream over the city and across the Nile, adding a hypnotic soundtrack to an exotic journey.

The architectural artifacts here, still impressive in their magnificent decay, speak across great swaths of time, thousands of years representing prosperity, regional dominance, political occupation, and inevitable decline and ruin. But the wonder of their making still reverberates through eons to the present, radiating from a force forever suspended in distant, lost time; a dimension both unique and mysterious and a profound legacy left us by the ancient children of the creator god Atum.

And as Shelley once pronounced:
My name is Ozymandias, king of kings:
Look on my works, ye Mighty, and despair!
Nothing beside remains. Round the decay
Of that colossal wreck, boundless and bare
The lone and level sands stretch far away.
—Ozymandias, 1818

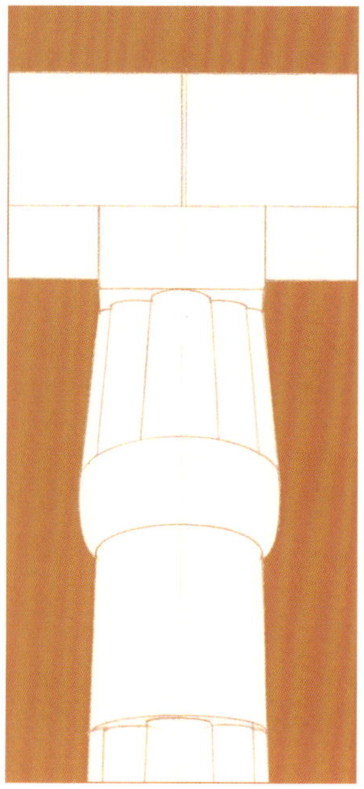

Closed Bud Capital

Lotus Blossom Capital

Palm Capital

Step Pyramid / Saqqara

Saqqara

DAY 1

SAQQARA PROVED TO BE our introduction to the landscapes of fierce heat and aridity that characterize the Saharan settings for the majority of Egyptian pyramids and temples. One wonders how they first conceived and later constructed anything in this sand-blasted, scorched-earth environment, much less the monuments that dot the terrain, scattered along the Nile River for hundreds of miles.

Images depicting the eroded and ancient profile of the great Step Pyramid at the center of this district give an impression of primeval, stolid antiquity, when in fact it represents a revolutionary leap forward in the development of a new and daring design language for royal monuments.

AMONG the hundreds of desert constructions erected by the pharaohs, none places one more deeply into the ancient, exotic world of the occult and the mysteries conceived by the Egyptian mind in antiquity than the royal necropolis at Saqqara, the funerary complex famous for the Step Pyramid of King Djoser. Its dimensions are impressive, a thirty-seven-acre compound of massive walls and structures that dominates the prospect of this desert plateau on the eastern edge of the Sahara, its ruins now and forever awash with sand.

Imhotep, the polymathic visionary and architect (in reality, if not in name) displayed remarkable ingenuity in this early effort to give physical expression to primitive imaginings regarding the transcendental nature of life after death and man's attempts to define a spiritual means to immortality. The divinity of the pharaoh, itself an assumption of a magical state of being, inspired one of the

Entrance Approach / Saqqara

world's first architects to create an imposing assertion of power and permanence in the magnificent Step Pyramid, a dense, monumental construction of solid masonry, intended to stand for all time, protecting the mummified deity king for eternity.

THE DISTANCE from present-day Cairo to Saqqara is less than twenty-five miles, but the transition requires a mental and a cultural leap of over 4,500 years to the remote 3rd Dynasty of the Old Kingdom. It stands as a seminal creation in the evolution of royal structures that would culminate with Khufu's Pyramid at the Giza necropolis.

As our vehicle nears the site, the remnants of this immense development rise from this indistinctive landscape in a spectacular array of structures, once imagined and created by both priest and pharaoh: temples, tombs, chapels, festival shrines, courts, and the great pyramid, its architectural and spiritual center. Within this massive perimeter wall, the rituals of daily god worship and animal mummification (including humans) took place in the rarefied atmosphere of the dead, now suspended in another dimension, being prepared by the living for a new life in eternity.

Once there, as we visually scan from north to south, the panorama takes in the remains of the once immense enclosure wall of ashlar stone that occupies the foreground. In the distance, behind the remains of the original wall and within the necropolis, the eroded structure of the chapels of the Heb-Sed Court and the celebrated Step Pyramid appear just above the mounds of rubble accumulated on this desert plain.

The arid dominance of brown, beige, and traces of yellow, which we will see in every part of our travels, are the dusty tones of antiquity with a subtle contrast among the surfaces of desert, tomb, and pyramid. A permutation of these colors in the overall palette of the scene defines this environment's visual character. Today, on our visit, the open desert is radiant with the scorching heat of midday, among the hottest sites we visited and without any significant shelter except under the covered colonnade at the entry.

From the drop-off point, we fan out over the tarmac, and then narrow down to enter the one, small door opening at the southwest corner of the extensive ancient perimeter enclosure. We cross the threshold, stepping into a world whose ancient mysteries are embodied in the sacred spaces of subterranean chambers and above-ground edifices dense with solid masonry.

Entrance Façade / Saqqara

Entrance and Step Pyramid / Saqqara

Partial Elevation of South Tomb / Saqqara

Architecture

ON THE APPROACH to the entrance, one is first struck by the sheer abstract force of what remains of the nearly thirty-five-foot-tall circumscribing stone enclosure wall (1,800 feet by 900 feet), architecturally characterized by simple, square-edged, vertical indentations etched out in shadow and marching in strict rhythm across the façade. The surface, shallow in profile and drab in color, is devoid of ornament and iconography and fittingly sober and mute, even morbid, in its effect. The repeated projections of equally spaced bays at the perimeter give the impression of a fortress, one to protect the living, rather than a tomb field to contain the dead.

Entry Colonnade

AT THE COMPLETION of the perimeter boundary, there were fifteen doors in the outer wall, fourteen false entrances and one actual access point—the same opening we pass through today. This small doorway takes us into a narrow but remarkable passage (approximately 22 feet wide by 225 feet long by 20 feet in height), rectangular in plan and enclosed by perimeter half walls that are open above. A straight interior path is defined by the rhythm of equally spaced columns on each side (twenty pairs), which run the length of the room. Sculpted to resemble string-bound papyrus bundles, these tapered supports bear a resemblance to classical Greek columns where verticality is also emphasized, but instead of the Grecian fluting created by curved indentations, the profile here is an outward bulge.

Each column is connected horizontally to an adjacent exterior wall so the effect is not that of a room of free-standing columns, but a series of shallow niches. As a distant precursor to the great hypostyle halls at later temples, one feels the same sensation of forward movement, but here the path is narrow and the dimensions smaller. On this constricted path, the visitor is inexorably carried along to the end, exiting into the vast outdoor space of the Great South Court, whose northern side is defined by the towering ziggurat-like pyramid.

From the colonnade we emerge from one corner of the complex that takes us into the blazing sun and the immense, open court—on the left is the ruin of a tomb wall whose parapet is embellished with apotropaic cobra figures, and to the right rises Djoser's Step Pyramid in the near distance. With a visual scan, moving from east to west, one starts to appreciate the enormity of the site and the variety of development.

Colonnade Entrance / Saqqara

Pyramid

PRIOR TO IMHOTEP'S great stylistic leap here, royalty was preserved in the mastaba building type: a single-story, windowless brick structure with a rectangular plan and battered outer walls, positioned over subterranean burial chambers. The form represented the primeval mound of the Earth to which all returned. We would see a number of these adjacent to the pyramid field at Giza.

At Saqqara, Imhotep altered the course of architecture by creating a new and original building type in the tiered profile of the step pyramid. The original mastaba here was square in plan and later added to vertically and horizontally, in stages, to eventually arrive at the finished Step Pyramid. In essence, the structure gives the appearance of six stacked mastabas, each one smaller than the one below to create a structure of solid masonry, 200 feet in height, with a profile of walls angling back at each level, somewhat like a squared-off wedding cake. The image suggested is that of a mountain, a man-made verisimilitude of nature in the flat, dry desert.

Step Pyramid from South Tomb / Saqqara

From this wall, the pyramid shows exactly on axis, therefore in pure profile. In this view, its mass wholly dematerializes, since nothing about it causes the mind's eye to supply it with any other sides. It seems to step back like a weightless stairway, mounting to the heavens. It is a flat folded plane, and it is climbing into the sky itself, carrying Djoser with it.

—Scully (1991, 27)

Colonnade Entrance Vestibule / Saqqara

With Imhotep's creation, we feel near the beginning of the "art of architecture," and it may defensibly be described as among the first structures, if not the first, to embody those qualities associated with a meaningful, complex art of building:

Permanence of materials (ashlar stone applied over a rough masonry structure)

Advanced construction techniques (the quarrying, transporting, and assembling of cyclopean stone blocks)

Symbolic reference (mountain and Earth symbol)

Monumentality (grandeur to reflect royal wealth and power)

Philosophy/religion (the pharaoh as deity)

Standing before its angular shape and massive bulk on this desert plateau, I could not make a direct reference to any stylistic or historical model. Here, there are no symbols or signs, no characters or images of religious or political association. The whole is one magnificent, primal abstraction of royal power, cultic fantasy, and relentless fate, stepping skyward in broad corrugations. The characteristics of its crude profile and the desert-colored rubble of its surface conjure up a scenario where the creator god Atum imagined the structure's primitive silhouette and willed it to rise from the desert floor in one eruptive convulsion. Saqqara's mausoleum was a brilliant extension of the common mastaba building type, here transformed into a new and radical expression of architecture.

This invention, the incipient precursor of the polyhedral structure with four equal triangular faces, proved to be a design aesthetic that would eventually reach its pinnacle in the Great Pyramid of Pharaoh Khufu.

Heb-Sed Court and Hall

TO THE CONTEMPORARY EYE, removing the small amount of ornament that graces the Heb-Sed Court and Hall buildings would result in a defensible "modern" structure. We sense this especially when moving from the great court to the east façade of the hall, where a tall wall extension of the last block curves along the path to encourage the visitor to engage with the stone forms of the complex. Simple square or rounded roof lines contribute to this feeling of simplicity.

Passing along the south end of the block, we enter the open, rectangular Heb-Sed Court where ceremonies were performed to commemorate the pharaoh's thirtieth year of reign and to mark a rejuvenation of his powers to rule. On the west side of the Heb-Sed Court, what appears to be a grouping of several contiguous chapel buildings are, in fact, spurious "dummy" buildings filled with solid masonry. Like a movie set, they served as stage and backdrop for the performance of rituals. On the east side of the building, there are low-walled forecourts in front of the chapels and two sets of long, shallowly angled steps rising to deep niches that may have once featured a statue of the pharaoh.

Where the Step Pyramid is mass-heavy and devoid of decorative detail, the false chapels are smaller in scale, articulated as individual entities and graced with delicate ornament. Like Grecian temples of stone, whose designs and details include references to earlier wooden constructions, the chapels here are also reminiscent of similar ancient worship structures in Egypt. For example, some of the individual pavilions are arched at the end façades, and some include delicate, carved reed and leaf ornament. On the west side of the Heb-Sed pavilions, there are additional chapel façades and the remnants of a structure featuring tapered columns with papyrus-like bundled stone ornament.

Step Pyramid from Colonnade Entrance / Saqqara

Step Pyramid from Heb-Sed Hall / Saqqara

Interior Corridor / Saqqara

East Façade: Heb-Sed Hall End Pavilion / Saqqara

The mysteries embodied within the walls of the Saqqara complex stand among Egypt's most ancient strivings to artistically express a quest for the divine through both art and architecture. In art there is the evolution of decorative refinement such as seen in the Heb-Sed Halls and related iconography; in architecture, there is the inchoate, yet profound leap forward of the Step Pyramid and its influence on future architectural style and civic monuments.

Step Pyramid / Saqqara

East Elevation: Heb-Sed Hall / Saqqara

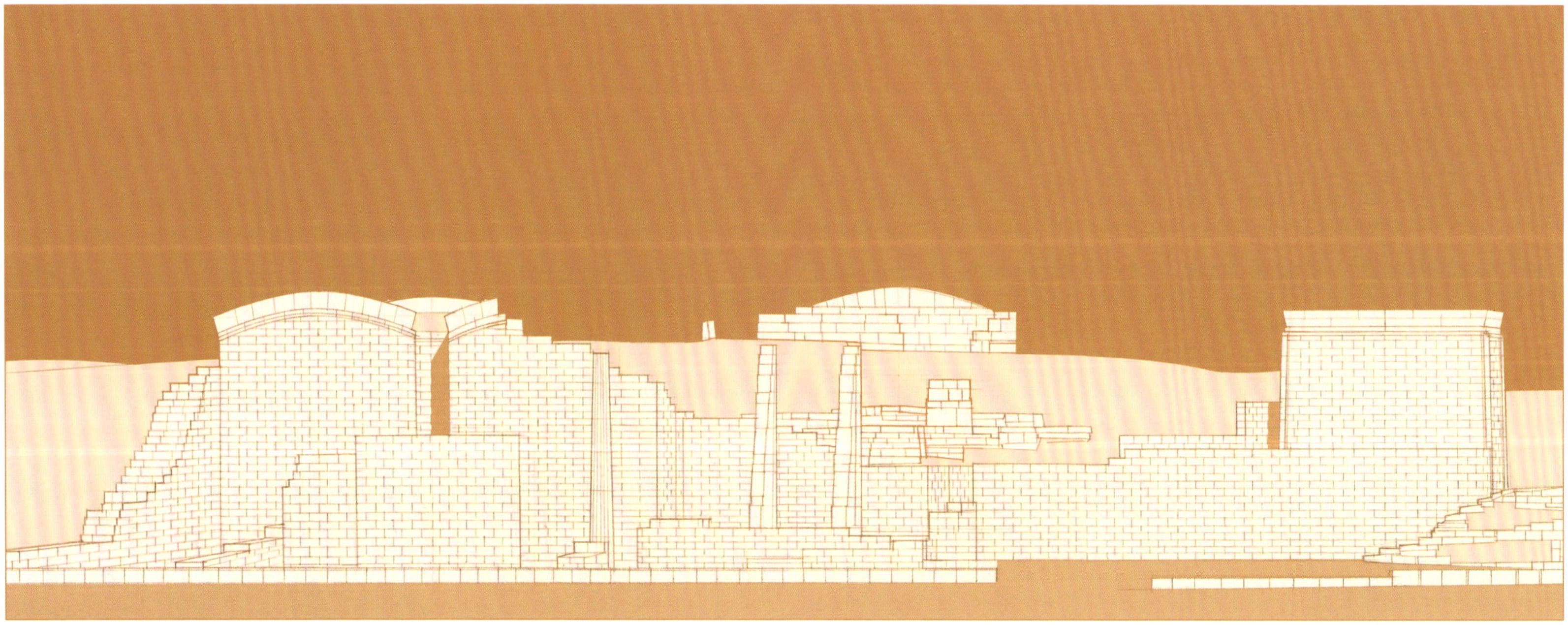

West Elevation: Heb-Sed Hall / Saqqara

East Façade Heb-Sed Hall / Saqqara

West Façade Heb-Sed Hall / Saqqara

Memphis

DAY 1

KNOWING LITTLE ABOUT THE SITE before our visit, we are surprised to find the artifacts on display in the small open-air museum from this civilization's first capital combining Upper and Lower Egypt to be relatively few and relatively modest. The splendors of ancient Memphis, Egypt's once stately capital, established 5,000 years ago at the nexus of the Nile and its delta, have all but evaporated under the harsh eye of Amun-Ra, the sun god.

This once resplendent city, a thriving and vital center of commerce, eventually lost its pre-eminence. Inevitably, the consequent loss of power and influence resulted in the city's demise, and the plundering of the buildings for construction material erased its presence over time.

Leaving our transport, we enter the grounds. To the left is a line of typical merchant kiosks, directly ahead sits a super-scaled statue of Ramesses II at the end of our vista and the alabaster Sphinx of Memphis in prone position occupies the middle ground.

To the right is a small, flat-roofed, two-story nondescript building housing the most impressive artifact at this site—a colossal remnant of a statue of Ramesses II lying face upward, occupying most of the ground floor area. The figure is in remarkably good condition, especially the head, chest, and torso. Because the statue is in a horizontal position on the pavilion floor, the visitor can move very close to the face, which is both beautiful and refined, while from the mezzanine level above, semi-open to the exterior, we have an excellent vantage point to take in the entire figure.

Exiting to the grounds, we inspect the alabaster Memphis Sphinx, which may have been among the line of statues once defining the approach to the Temple of Ptah (the creator god of Memphis); it reclines at the nominal center of the open space. At approximately ninety tons and with a length of twenty-six feet and height of thirteen feet, it is a significant, although not commanding, object as it looks down the site to the statue of the standing Ramesses II.

The simply sculpted human head of the sphinx is adorned with a typical headdress, including the uraeus (Egyptian cobra) crowning the forehead, and the features of the face, as customary, show no strong emotion as it fulfills its role as protector of the temple. It does, however, provide a well-scaled artifact as backdrop for tourists' photos.

Approximately 200 feet beyond the sphinx is a free-standing colossus of Ramesses II from the New Kingdom. It is a typical representation: Ramesses stands tall with arms down against the body, stepping forward with the left leg and foot. Equipped with a false beard and the simple crown of Upper Egypt, it appears to be emerging from the vertical slab of stone. At over thirty feet in height, it impressively establishes the end of the vista at one edge of the site.

Among the relics in this open-air setting stand a chipped stone stela, eroded column capitals, minor sculptures, and miscellaneous fragments, the historic detritus of a once radiant city.

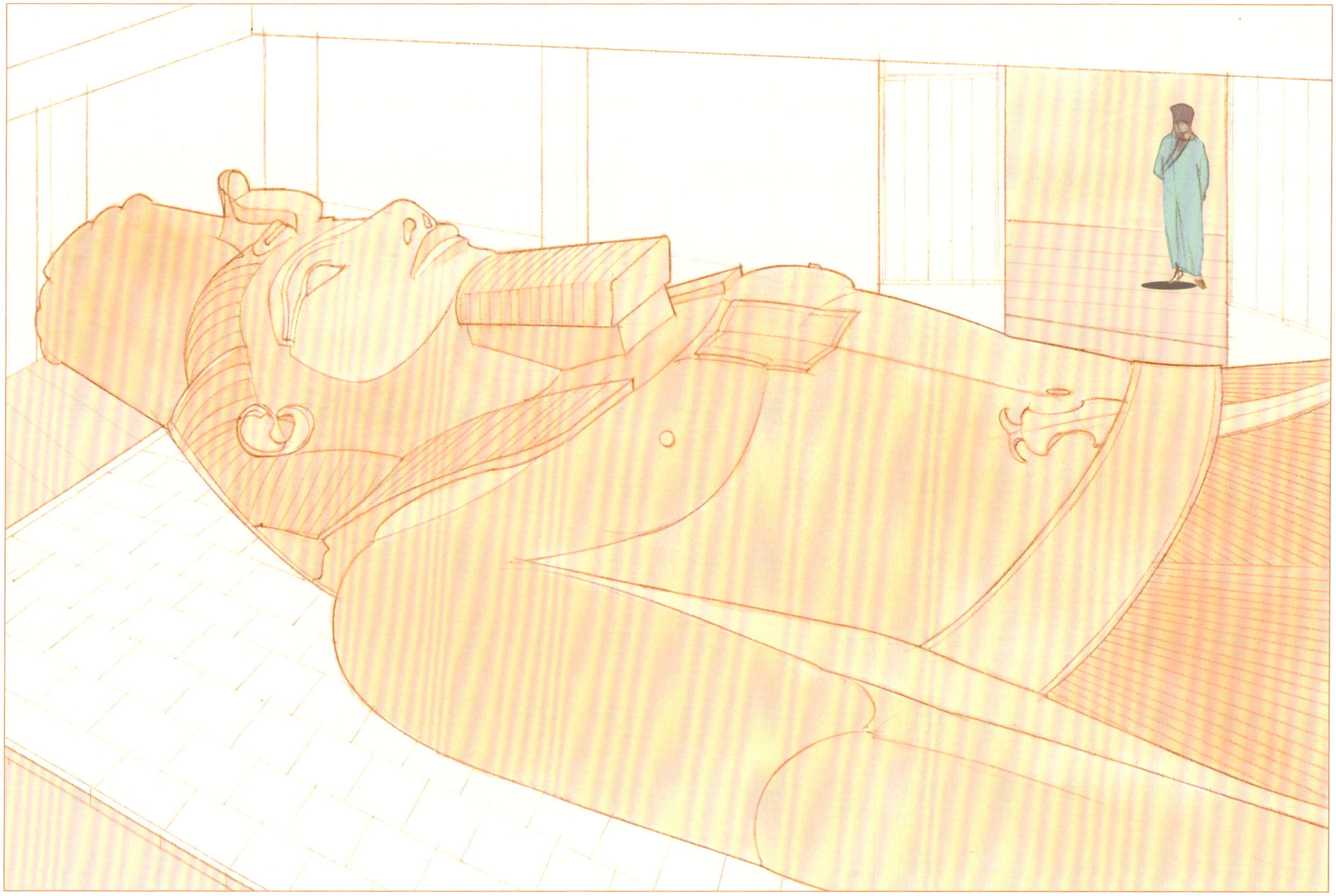

Ramesses II / Memphis

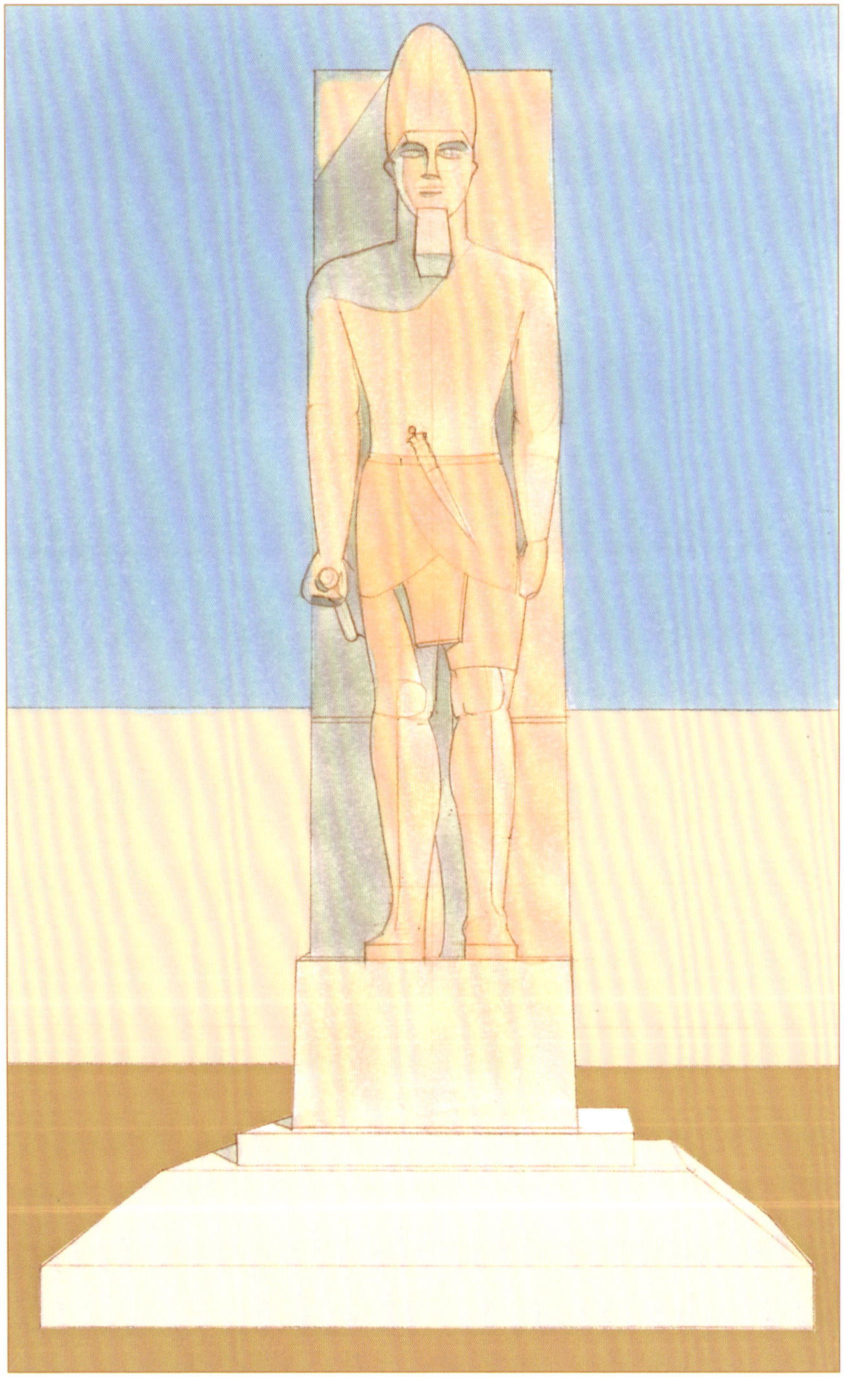

Ramesses II / Memphis

Sphinx of Memphis / Memphis

Dahshur

DAY 2

TODAY WE ARE TRAVELING WEST, moving away from the sad disorder of present-day Cairo, passing dusty townscapes, dry canals, and railway tracks, crossing over the "green ribbon" of the Nile into the Sahara and a vista defined only by the flat horizon line between desert and sky. Our destination is the site of the first true pyramid to be constructed in Egypt. Turning south into the pyramid field at Dahshur, driving through a sandy plateau on a paved stretch of road curving subtly in an elongated S-shape, we pass the Red Pyramid on our left, and moving on in a gentle arc, we then see the Black Pyramid to the east before arriving at the parking area closest to the provocatively titled Bent Pyramid, its slanted shape in the distance, as our initial destination.

This is the desert setting of Egypt's first true pyramidal mausoleum. King Menes and a future line of pharaohs established their royal necropolises in this place, running north/south on the west bank of the Nile and just outside the natural line currently delineating verdant agriculture from barren desert.

Known as the Memphite Necropolis, this swath of desert includes, moving south from Giza, the great Pyramid of Khufu and its satellite structures, including the Great Sphinx; Saqqara, among the oldest burial sites with the revolutionary Step Pyramid of Djoser; and the pyramid field here at Dahshur.

Although we are not very far from the greenish flow of the Nile (just over a mile), the setting is a lunar landscape of barren aridity: a desiccated Saharan setting of compacted earth, sand, and clay, devoid of visible life as far as the eye can see (although near the Red Pyramid is an abandoned rusted-out kiosk surrounded by trash, Coke bottles, and a gas can, left unattended in the sun).

A panoramic view of the site, moving from north to south, as seen through a haze of pollution and sand hanging in the

Bent Pyramid + Red Pyramid / Dahshur

Bent Pyramid / Dahshur

heated air, takes in the Red, Black, and Bent Pyramids, with the three forming a right triangle in plan. Additional eroded stone "mounds" and miscellaneous structures fill in the scene set against the backdrop of low sand dunes as the desert extends, virtually unpopulated, for thousands of miles to the west and hundreds of miles to the south.

The enclosure walls and associated structures (shrines, altars, temples, and causeways) of each pyramid are mostly gone, seemingly swept away by blasting walls of blown sand and unchecked human spoliation. Each pyramid body, however, still contains some of the original tomb chambers and passages above and below the desert plateau.

We exit the vehicle, leaving us about 700 feet from the Bent Pyramid, and take shelter in a tiny, wooden pavilion, open on all sides. It sits alone in this vast landscape and offers a small trapezoid of slowly moving shade before we venture out into the desert.

Bent Pyramid / Dahshur

Architecture

OF THE THREE REMAINING PYRAMIDS at Dahshur, the Bent and the Red are believed to have been built under the Pharaoh Sneferu (father of Khufu), while the Black Pyramid was constructed under King Amenemhat III. Each now has a distinctive body profile: Bent Pyramid (faceted), Red Pyramid (true triangular faces, but now with a slightly irregular outline), and Black Pyramid (atavistic, eroded mountain form). To some extent, all the structures here have been reduced by pillage, environment, or both, but the Red Pyramid still retains a good deal of its outer cladding and significant areas of finished stone exist on the Bent Pyramid. One imagines how the physical relationship among the three tombs here, when completed, would have established a context of significant desert architecture, now lessened by the passage of time and erosion.

Bent Pyramid

THE DISTINCTIVE AND UNIQUE profile of the Bent Pyramid stands out against the sky, with the rubble of a small mound to the south, located behind it; the Red Pyramid is to the north; and the Black Pyramid (with its eroded mountain profile) is in the distance, visible through a softened blur of vaporous heat.

Architecturally, the original design of the Bent Pyramid (intended to be a pure tetrahedron, most believe) was a significant leap forward when compared with Saqqara's Step Pyramid, itself a remarkable, imaginative fantasy of stacked mastabas. At Dahshur, the first pyramid was to consist of four triangular façades on a square base converging at the apex of the building in a true pyramidal shape.

The science of structural engineering did not exist in ancient Egypt—construction practices were, for the most part, based on empirical data gained from numerous successes and numerous collapses. In the case of the Bent Pyramid, material failure supposedly occurred midway through the construction, requiring an adjustment in the angle of the slope from approximately 54° to approximately 42°. This alteration resulted in a multi-angled profile, with the top portion tilting sharply to the apex. Because of this defect, it is now famous for its dual-angled cross section, and, despite the fact that it has eight faces instead of four, it still bears the architectural distinction of being the first pyramid where four faces converge to a point at the top of the building. (Some believe, however, that this "break" was part of the original design.)

In its current state, the remaining outer stone cladding forms a jagged outline on the pyramid's body, with its inner core of stones revealed as a jumble of irregular, tumbling blocks. Coupled with a variegation of surface colors, the body mass is now a great, hulking aggregate of finished and unfinished stones—more giant scarab than simulated mountain.

Other smaller satellite structures exist, but in soft, deteriorated mounds, while on the east side, the ruin of a chapel consisting of vertical stone supports, a stone roof, and stela fragments remains, but in very poor condition.

On the day of our visit, three men and a camel were taking refuge from the midday sun in the ample shade of the ruin, and, as a respite from the heat and glare, we joined them, resting prior to our trek around the faceted tomb and subsequent march to the mysterious Black Pyramid.

Bent Pyramid + Red Pyramid / Dahshur

Black Pyramid

TO THE EAST, at a distance of slightly less than a mile from the Bent Pyramid, is the dark pile of the Black Pyramid, built by Pharaoh Amenemhat III. Poorly engineered and constructed with a mud masonry core, the loss of its exterior casing of stone has left it vulnerable to decay. It is now an eroded mass of clay and mud brick. The asymmetrical shape consists of an irregular, dark masonry mass rising from a tapered, mountain-shaped body of rubble and accumulated sand. Its evocation is currently that of a natural, eroded formation, not a man-made structure. Its color and shape promote a feeling of mystery, and its irregular, nonsymmetrical silhouette would not look out of place in the desert of the American West.

Black Pyramid / Dahshur

Red Pyramid: Pyramidion Capstone / Dahshur

Red Pyramid

KING SNEFERU, in the thirteenth year of his reign, began construction on the Red Pyramid (so-named because of the reddish limestone core). It is the largest structure at Dahshur, and has the distinction of being the world's first true pyramid, still in excellent condition with part of the interior chambers open to the public. The loss of its outer casing means the profile, similar to that of the Giza pyramids, is stepped at each stone and not uniformly smooth. The surface is now dull, not brilliantly reflective as it would have been at its completion.

Access to the interior is through an opening on the north façade, and a series of low corridors connect the exterior to various chambers, two of which (at forty and fifty feet in height) offer considerable interest with corbeled ceilings of stone, creating an elongated, stepped gable shape space in section. A discovered pyramidion capstone, thought to have once crowned the structure, is on display outside its entrance.

Small Pyramid / Dahshur

Chapel Ruins / Dahshur

An aura of mystery defined the antique world within the decaying walls of Saqqara. Dahshur presented another level of development with the relationship of pyramid to pyramid across the open desert. We could sense the presence of Ma'at (representing the cosmic balance) in the Red Pyramid's perfect contours as a spectral aura bounded by rational geometry. Next, we would travel on to Giza and its expansive precinct where the structures reach greater heights and the mysteries run deeper.

Giza

DAY 3

AT A HEIGHT OF OVER FORTY STORIES, Khufu's tomb at Giza expands vertically and horizontally from the desert floor as we approach by auto: a massive triangular shape dominating our perspective with a presence as formidable as any precipitous mountain formation. Familiarity with Giza through printed and electronic media will not prepare one for the sheer breadth and weight of this mountain of stonework.

Everything around the pyramids is dwarfed by the magnitude of the structures here. Moving about the site in the midday heat (shading my camera to prevent spontaneous combustion), one imagines the experience at the time when all the structures were newly completed: the flawless, triangle of the pyramid as a stunning symbol of the occult set against the resplendent rays of Amun-Ra the sun god; the Great Sphinx, polychromatic and daunting; and the mastabas, sharp-edged, shaping the encircling spaces—all held in perfect suspension by Ma'at's magical balancing force.

THIS IS THE SITE of the ancient world's most ambitious building effort—a vast royal necropolis where construction activity spanned hundreds of years and numerous dynasties, established on a high, sand-blown expanse of south-facing limestone and compacted desert located between the Nile and the Sahara and now contiguous with the metropolis of Cairo. This once featureless expanse of desiccated desert was transformed into one of the most recognizable places in the modern world with its distinctive pyramid field of nine tombs (three large pharaoh pyramids associated with Khufu, Khafre and Menkaure and six smaller pyramids) and the Great Sphinx, plus the ruins of numerous ancillary structures of stone, including mastabas, temples, and rock-cut tombs.

Even when compared to the grandeur and brilliance of Karnak's temple or the surreal magnificence of Abu Simbel, Giza, in its enormity of scale and its strata of dynastic remains, still stands as Egypt's greatest and most monumental achievement. It expresses the ancient Egyptians' deepest, most profound belief in an afterlife and their dedication to securing a path to perpetuity for their king and pharaoh. The temples and pyramids, among the largest and most difficult construction efforts of all time, are enduring monuments to a system of transcendental beliefs centered around the workings of gods and their influence on preserving the stability of the universe.

Formal entry to the Giza necropolis in antiquity was from the east, accessed from an extension of the Nile. Each of the individual pyramid complexes consisted of four major structures: a valley temple (at the river's edge), a causeway (an enclosed path from the valley temple to the funerary temple), a funerary temple (contiguous with the pyramid), and the pyramid itself.

In addition to these great pyramids, two extensive mastaba cemeteries are located immediately east and west of Khufu's tomb, and three small pyramids, now heavily eroded, are situated just south of the Menkaure's tomb. Last, an additional three small queen pyramids, also in various stages of wear, are located east of Khufu's tomb.

Adjacent to the causeway entrance leading to the Pyramid of Khafre reclines the Great Sphinx, once rendered in vivid colors and formerly the world's largest sculpture: an awe-inspiring, intimidating figure looming on the horizon. It remains the grandest mythic depiction of the supernatural merging of man into beast (or beast into man, possibly), rendered in monolithic stone and sculpted in situ.

Like the Oedipal sphinx of Grecian Thebes, Giza Plateau's "desert monster" stands as the inscrutable and mute gatekeeper surveying the flow of visitors admitted to this greatest of royal pyramid fields.

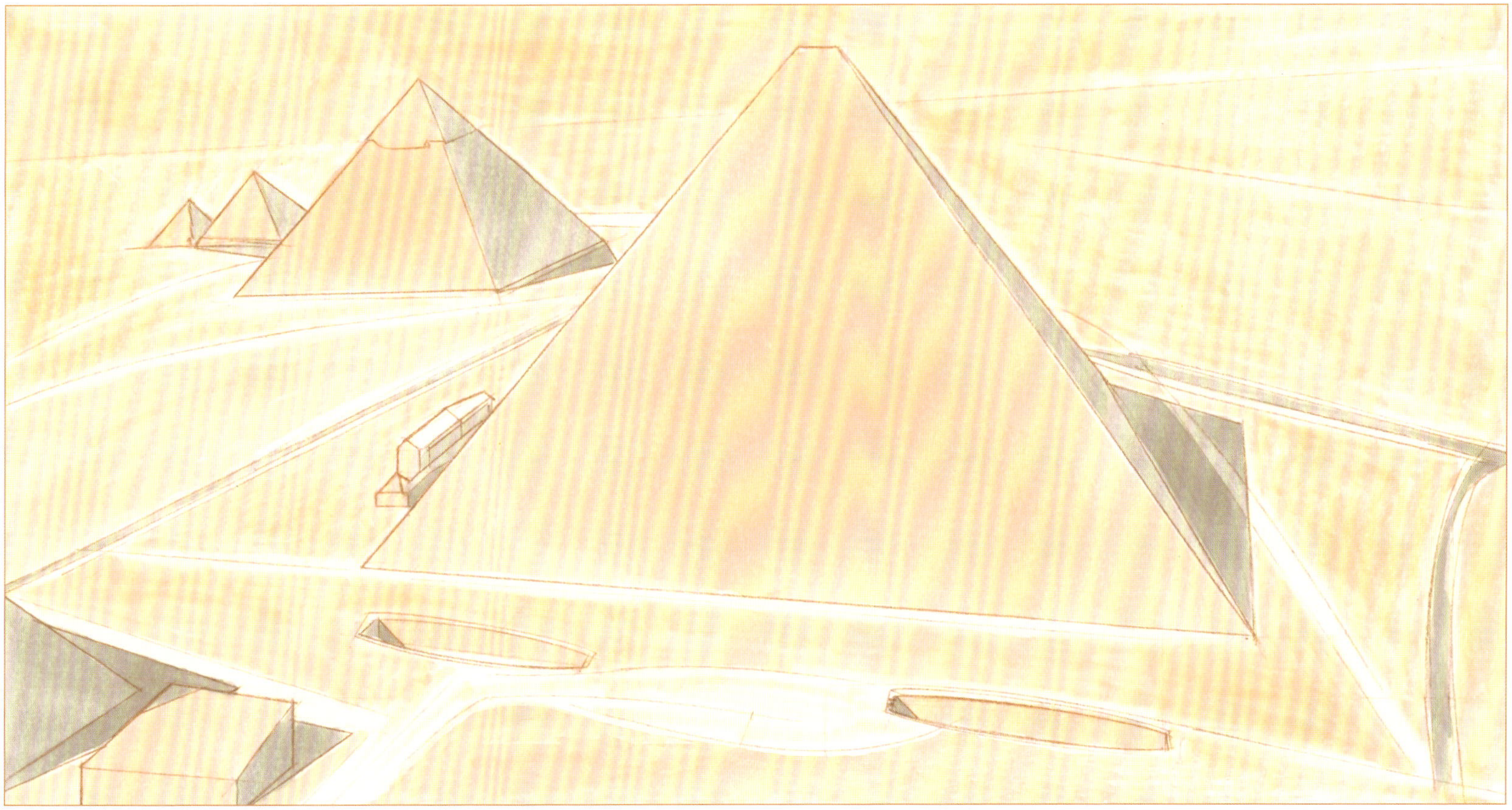

Pyramids / Giza

Originally, all the faces of the pyramid at Giza were sheathed in gleaming white limestone, blindingly bright, sending out reflections far across the plain. The cult was of Ra, the sun and the pyramids were indeed transformed into pure sun's rays, pure light.
—Scully (1991, 27)

Site

SO ON THIS CLOUDLESS AFTERNOON, in the midday heat, we move into the extensive shade of what was the tallest building in the world for over 4,000 years. Viewed from the north to the south, from Khufu's pyramid to Menkaure's, the corners of all three big pyramids are in near alignment, setting up a stunning relationship: they appear to be the same pyramid moving away into the desert, periodically captured as an image in perspective. This ambiguity among the foreground (the Great Pyramid), the middle-ground (Pyramid of Khafre), and the background (Pyramid of Menkaure) at a distance of over half a mile makes for an interesting, seemingly shifting relationship of these massive pieces.

This dynamic interaction gives us the sense of moving between sharply rising topography, the ground ascending abruptly from relatively flat earth to sharp verticality and the sky. The geometric "mountain form" is abstracted and rudimentary, and its simplicity of shape belies the nearly insurmountable challenge of construction in this manner and at this scale. As an example of the artist expanding the bounds of expression through engineering, it remains among architecture's greatest accomplishments.

Later, after inspecting the ruins of pyramids and mastabas, we move to the opposite side of this site and stand before the Great Sphinx. Looking from east to west (the longitudinal axis of its body), with the ruins of the Valley Temple of Khafre in the foreground, the three great pyramids take on a very different character. Here, the plateau rises behind the disfigured face of the massive sculpture, and in the background the pointed tops of the three largest pyramids punctuate the skyscape from north to south, rising to varying heights. From this vantage point, it is impossible to determine the actual size of each (are they ten stories tall or thirty?), and this ambiguity lends an added element of mystery and power to their effect on the landscape.

Architecture / Pyramids

NUMEROUS CULTURES have built pyramids or pyramid-like structures for worship or as public monuments. In Mesoamerica, the limestone-clad pyramids were stepped and terraced with wide stairs rising steeply to the temple structure at the top, accommodating access for ritualistic ceremony. The effect was a highly articulated structure, "boxy" and primitive in profile, its rough textures making the mountain metaphorical image more overt. Although man-made, several seem to have pushed skyward from the jungle in one massive upheaval, rising above the tree line toward heaven and relating, in silhouette, to mountainous terrain in the distance.

The stepped ziggurats of the Middle East were constructed out of brick and also have a less refined, more hand-made appearance. Here, too, the monuments were massive with plans whose

Valley Temple / Giza

perimeters varied in outline and with sections of wall that flared out in a buttress-like thickening of structure. The effect here was also primordial, like a rugged, truncated mountain or hill with wide masonry stairs to a top ritual platform for public ceremony.

In contrast, the great tomb of Khufu represents the Egyptian pyramid in its most evolved state—four perfectly flat triangular planes, sharp-edged and exact. There is nothing remotely "primitive" in its profile, and, because it was not a structure of worship, there is no ornamental or iconographic signs or symbolic associations—no stairs rising to the apex. It is a single, man-made mausoleum for the ruling pharaoh, constructed from stone material quarried nearby in chromatic sympathy with its sun-bleached desert setting.

As Vincent Scully observed, the solar reflection from the polished stone surfaces would have "dematerialized" the structure into a blinding, radiant emanation of the sun god, channeled through the mummified remains of the pharaoh (Scully 1991, 27). Overwhelming to the human eye, it would have inspired belief in the unimpeachable omnipotence and divinity of Amun-Ra.

Architecturally, the Egyptians also created the perfect building form. With all façades meeting at a single point, the architect was not faced with the challenge of how to terminate the building where it meets the sky. There are no balustrades, fascias, or moldings; instead, the four faces converge to one point, which has no dimension, and the mass disappears.

Pyramids / Giza

Khufu's Great Pyramid

THE GREAT PYRAMID OF KHUFU is a monument whose iconicity is universally acknowledged both in our popular culture and in academic circles. In magnitude, precision of workmanship, and difficulty of construction, it remains a wonder, even today. At the nominal center of its massive amplitude of over two million megalithic stone blocks, an occult force, according to religious belief, reanimated lifeless, earthly matter as it merged with the deity king, the pharaoh-god Khufu. The enshrined king, transformed by solar rays spreading from the pyramidion down, became one with the god of the sun, Amun-Ra.

The effort to construct a pyramid of this size, one tomb for one man, a nexus for the intersection of the divine and the mundane, lasted over twenty years. How the pyramids, the Great Pyramid especially, were constructed, the exact means and methods for quarrying, transporting, and assembling stone blocks weighing 2.5 tons with precision hundreds of feet above the desert, still remains a mystery after 4,500 years.

Pyramid of Queen Henutsen / Giza

Other Giza Pyramids

PHARAOH KHAFRE'S TOMB (2570 BC): The second largest of the Giza pyramids is supported on a base of pink granite with the remainder clad in limestone. Commissioned by the son of Khufu, it stands at 450 feet.

Pharaoh Menkaure's Tomb (2511 BC): The smallest of the major pyramids here (its base is a mere quarter of the two larger pyramids), it is sheathed in limestone except for the first sixteen stone courses, which are granite.

In addition, there are also six Giza "satellite" pyramids: three queen pyramids (Henutsen, Meritites I, and Hetepheres I) located just east of Khufu's tomb, and three pyramids located just south of Menkaure's, all in a state of advanced deterioration. While relatively small, as "miniatures" of the great pyramids, they create a context for the larger structures and define the extents of the site, east and south.

Mastaba + Pyramid of Khafre / Giza

Valley Temple Passage / Giza

Sphinx

WITH THE HEAD OF A MAN and the body of a lion, the Great Sphinx at Giza is a startling oddity. As one of the world's largest sculptures, it is a commanding presence at nearly 250 feet in length and six stories in height. Cut directly from the limestone Giza Plateau, its leonine animality is emphasized by the characteristic reclining pose of its species. Its face has been disfigured, so the person (a pharaoh, presumably) depicted is in question.

Known as the "father of terror" (Abu al-Hol) to the Arabs, it stood as the guardian of the entrance to the Giza Necropolis. It is said to have spoken to King Tuthmosis IV in a dream, commenting on the sand gathered around its body and the effect on its ability to protect the tombs. Today, the sand has been removed and the sculpture sits in a very large, rectangular depression, a rail-less drop of thirty feet that allows the visitor to view, with great caution, all sides of the figure. It seems to hold less terror today and remains a popular spot for gathering and posing for photographs.

Great Sphinx / Giza

Great Sphinx / Giza

Mastaba Ruin / Giza

Great Sphinx / Giza

Entrance of Queen Meresankh III Tomb / Giza

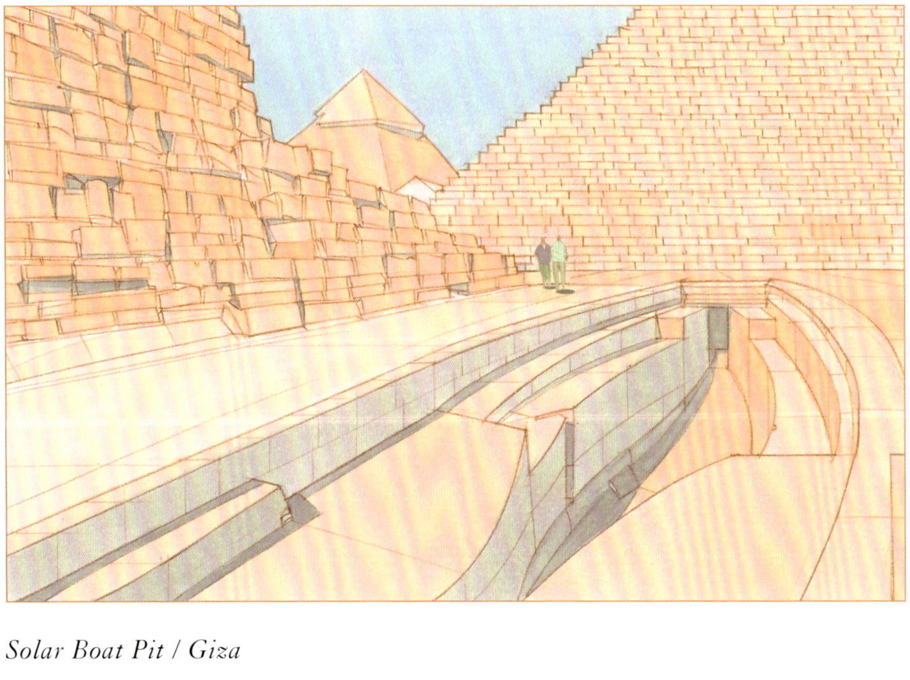

Solar Boat Pit / Giza

YET ALL IS NOT MASSIVE ABSTRACTION AT GIZA. As a contrast, Khufu's delicately fashioned wooden "solar boat" is on display in an ultra-modern, 20th-century pavilion of faceted metal and glass (curiously resembling a futuristic spacecraft, which may be intentional). The pavilion sits somewhat awkwardly adjacent to the Great Pyramid, parallel to one triangular face. In 1954, the unassembled boat (in over 1,200 pieces), meant for Khufu's journey through the afterlife, was discovered almost by chance in a pit outside the pyramid. It took over twelve years to reassemble.

Upon entering the pavilion, every visitor must place coverings over each shoe to reduce floor wear. After passing through some galleries of models and exhibits, we enter a multistory open space with the now assembled boat positioned in the middle, supported on metal columns. Within the space, walkways are suspended as "bridges," so it is possible to have views of the entire vessel. It is an impressive and beautiful example of superb Egyptian craftsmanship.

Additional structures, constructed on a smaller scale, include other tombs and numerous eroded mastabas set in rows. The mastaba tomb of Queen Meresankh III, located southeast of the Great Pyramid, is graced with an entry porch that is especially beautiful in its simplicity and ideal in proportion. The battered stone façade, at least what is left of it, is interrupted by an indented entrance, headed above with a simple lintel and a shallow cavetto molding. Supporting the lintel are two round columns with block capitals and short, round bases; the whole, still beautiful and inspiring in its ruined state.

Solar Boat Pavilion / Giza

Solar Boat / Giza

At nearly any time of day, the Giza Plateau is vibrant with activity: hundreds of tourists emptying out of buses and autos and then moving in all directions. As is typical of such sites, there are numerous vendors (the descendants of pharaohs and priests) with wares strung out along the sand in ragged lines of carpets and merchandise, selling Egyptian mythic trinkets, camel rides, and cold drinks and posing with travelers for a fee, all beneath the eye of the Great Sphinx.

Karnak

DAY 4

FOR THE TRAVELER, the word "Karnak" invokes images of Egyptian exotica and desert mysteries: temples of great mass and darkened chambers of incantations and magic. It stands among the largest religious complexes ever built, a dramatic mise-en-scène populated with huge freestanding columns, the statuary of men and gods and animal figures arrayed as lines of sphinxes: a magnificent backdrop for pageantry, festival, and the worship of their deities.

Starting with a single structure and ending with a massive precinct of worship constructed over a period of approximately 1,300 years, Karnak Temple was dedicated to the greatest of the deities: Amun; Muut, his consort; and their son Khonus.

WE WALK FROM OUR TRANSPORT into the expansive paved plaza and turn ninety degrees to face the majestic entrance into what is one of the greatest achievements of the pharaohs: Karnak Temple. The time is near midday under a cloudless sky, and, as we approach the wide portal opening, flanked by a pair of pylons, the massive façade seems afloat on the vaporous, heated waves of air shimmering off the reflective pavement. With a crowd of hundreds descending on the site, the foreground is a plane of constantly shifting, multicolored patterns moving toward the slot between the unfinished towers at its entry point. Approaching the threshold to the complex, the converging crowds coalesce in the last 100 feet of a sphinx-bordered allée, axial with the sanctuary beyond. Each massive, unfinished pylon towers above the site, and the surge forward, of which we are willing participants, has the biblical sweep and the visual incident of Noah loading the Great Ark.

Temple Entrance / Karnak

Hypostyle Hall / Karnak

Hypostyle Hall Entrance from Great Court / Karnak

Temple Courtyard / Karnak

This extensive complex consists of ten pylons, several temples, numerous obelisks, barque stations, living quarters, and a sacred lake. It was a veritable city unto itself, but with just one significant purpose: the systematic management of god-worship and the staging of propitiation rituals of veneration, including supplications using magical prayers and spells.

Amun (later combined with the sun god Ra as Amun-Ra), one of the conjectured "creator deities," worshiped here as the king of gods, was, in certain myths, depicted as the progenitor of the physical world. According to one version, Amun magically conceived himself by supernatural conjuring and then took his place as the supreme god in the universe. The size and extent of this vast construction is a reflection of the importance of this deity force in Egyptian life.

Once inside the circumscribing enclosure wall of the compound, there are no views to the outside world, so the feeling of a rarefied, "other worldly" atmosphere is firmly established. The precinct is dense with structures, and the close relationship of flat and sloped walls without windows establishes a feeling of "pure architecture," unencumbered by expressed function. Within these great and thick walls, the feeling of shelter is patent, and the spaces are evocative vessels of filtered light in varying degrees of bright sun and dark shadow.

Hypostyle Hall: Bud + Bell Capitals / Karnak

But Amun's temple is all vegetable growth of river plants, while a current like that of the Nile flows from the narrow darkness of his sanctuary outward to court after court, hall after hall, added over generations.
—Scully (1991, 32)

Architecture / Temple

AT THE ENTRANCE TO THE KARNAK COMPLEX, the drably colored, unfinished façades of the paired entry pylons, originally designed to be approximately 100-feet high, bristle with the texturing shadows of unfinished stonework, appearing slightly out of alignment. It is an appropriately scaled introduction to this vast network of buildings.

Amun's Great Court is the first space we enter after moving through the double pylons (numbered 1 and 2). It is immense in size, filled with an imposing variety of architectural elements and structures (temples to Ramesses III and Seti II, plus freestanding lines of columns) that define the margins of the space and the symmetrical processional path to the Sanctuary of Amun. One must be reminded of the highly chromatic painted figures and hieroglyphics that once animated nearly every image here. Currently, most of that coloring, aside from some areas sheltered from the elements, is now faded down to the limestone.

Between the entry pylons and the hypostyle hall are the remains of the Kiosk of Taharqa, a station where the cultic barque stopped on its pilgrimage to other temples. This open structure of freestanding columns and "knee walls" would have dominated the entire center of this vast open court. A fabric-roofed pavilion with a rectangular plan, the space was defined by ten 60-foot tall columns with open papyrus capitals, connected at the base with low partitions to shelter the deity while in transit. Today, what remains is one entire column, five column stubs of varying heights and ten bases. Even with the majority of the superstructure missing, we still have a sense of the majestic presence this ancient "baldachino"-like structure would have imposed on the space.

Next, moving through what would have been the second set of pylons in the procession to the sanctuary, we are in the ruins of the Great Hypostyle Hall, among the most famous and awe-inspiring spaces from the ancient (or modern) world. The room is a veritable

Taharqa Kiosk Column / Karnak

Hypostyle Hall / Karnak

forest of massive columns (135) arranged in nine rows, the central twelve columns with papyrus capitals rising to over seventy feet in height, the balance being crowned with bud-styled capitals. It has been suggested that the hall is an allegory in stone with the space representing the Nile and its underwater environment. The grid of tapering columns and their capitals refers to reeds growing in the marshes along its riverbed, and the spectacular volume of space, at one time dimly lit from above by clerestory windows between supports, is the watery setting. Movement can be characterized as the cult statue "flowing" to and from the sanctuary in its barque, symbolically merging with the Nile as it exits the Amun complex or, when on route to the Mortuary Temple of Hatshepsut, actually crossing the river.

We enter the hall and are overwhelmed by the magnitude of the columns soaring through the high, expansive volume of the hall. The most striking visual effect during daytime is the dramatic quality of intense sunlight creating shadows that slash through the space, distorting around columns and falling as irregular, ever-changing patterns on the floor. Today, this light-filled room is in extreme contrast to its spatial quality in 1100 BC. At that time, it was a towering and mysterious volume of dark enclosure, with scant illumination from thin clerestory slits above and only fire light below. Every surface was highly polychromatic with hieroglyphics, geometric patterning and images covering every surface in a profusion of color and implied motion. Standing in the space, one can imagine the procession transporting the cult deity through this impressive array of pillars with gods and symbols appearing and disappearing as the members moved slowly through each space. Now, all we can do is join the rest of the travelers and look up in wonder, inspired by a spatial experience like no other in the world.

Continuing our movement toward the sanctuary, we move through the multiple layers of additional pylons, courts, and halls that take us to the oldest part of the of the complex: the original

Hypostyle Hall / Karnak

temple of the Middle Kingdom containing the sanctuary worship space. Here, at the center of the temple body, within concentric layers of stone, in a setting both hermetic and darkly mystifying, rites were conducted in the setting of a man-made state of simulated night with priests conjuring the forces of Ma'at. Each day was a day of conflict between the forces of order and the forces of chaos, and the temple was fashioned and equipped to provide physical and spiritual protection to the resident deity. The small original structure was later expanded over time and eventually encircled by other buildings in this vast institution.

Adjacent to and on axis with the sanctuary is the somewhat intact structure of the Great Festival Hall of Tuthmosis III (looking surprisingly "modern" in its ruined state) with its distinctive interior tapered pillars (reminiscent of Minoan tapered piers). Like those of the Greeks, there is (now faded) painted horizontal banding in blue and red colors on many columns, and the coffered ceiling also retains pockets of faded paint as well.

The balance of this part of Karnak is a field of ruins defined by vestiges of walls at varying heights, thicknesses, and stages of erosion. Also scattered through this area are a number of statues, some seated or standing in typical Osiriform pose (arms crossed with the crook and the flail pressed up against the chest), the whole looking somewhat like a great antique salvage yard.

Exiting this mass of super rubble and moving west, we now face the Sacred Lake, a fairly large body of water (250 feet x 400 feet), important for the priests' ablutions and as a stage setting for the enactment of mythic tales.

Temple View / Karnak

Seven Doors: Temple of Osiris Hek-Djet / Karnak

Festival Hall of King Tuthmosis III / Karnak

Festival Hall of King Tuthmosis III / Karnak

After sundown, when Amun-Ra has descended to the netherworld and the day has been consumed by the night goddess Nut, the mystique of cultic Karnak returns as a remarkable and inscrutable silhouette of great irregular masses and needle-shaped obelisks, set against the African sky. It is one imposing, massive god-shaped pile, ambiguous and full of wonder, mysterious and now abandoned.

Statue of Amun / Karnak

Temple Corridor with Gate of Nectanebo I / Karnak

Festival Hall of King Tuthmosis III / Karnak

Luxor

DAY 5

WE ARRIVE AT LUXOR by boat late in the day and dock directly across from the temple; Karnak is about two miles to the north. Each complex is an oasis of ruins set on the edge of an anonymous townscape. These two temple precincts are among the most visited historic sites anywhere, and after exploring Karnak, our expectations for Luxor are high. The complex is significantly smaller than Karnak, idiosyncratic in layout and orientation, and we need to be reminded of the difference in what an ancient Egyptian would have seen versus what we now see: a roofless ruin, stripped of its evocative, mysterious space, whose architectural peculiarities have been multiplied by built impositions over time.

TODAY, THE ONCE BRILLIANT CAPITAL, known as Thebes under various pharaohs, is a collage of boxy, muted beige buildings—anonymous architecture, four to six stories in height, that extends for blocks in all directions.

In Luxor, as in other places in Egypt, the ground floor of the town's buildings is typically mercantile space, selling and bargaining everything from McDonald's to exotic spices, with the upper floors used for lodging. At night, when we visit the temple, the streetscape is alive with an iridescent glow pouring out of painted teal-blue colored interiors under fluorescent lighting, garishly punctuating the darkness around these dimly lit urban blocks across from the former residence of Egypt's greatest deity.

Opposite the Luxor McDonald's stand the massive ruins of the temple complex started by Amenhotep III and continued by Tutankh-amun and Ramesses II. Now encircled by tarmac and automotive traffic, the precinct sits on a paved urban island between the city and the Nile.

Temple Elevation / Luxor

Temple Entrance View: Ramesses II Court / Luxor

Temple Entrance + Colonnade of Amenhotep III / Luxor

Temple View from Nile River / Luxor

Court of Ramesses II with Kiosk / Luxor

In distinct contrast to the majority of Egyptian temples, the axis runs north/south, parallel to the river, and the complex, adjacent to the water's edge at the completion of its construction, is now about 150 feet from our docked boat. The remnants of an allée, once lined with ram-headed sphinxes that connected Luxor Temple to the Karnak precinct, are still visible.

Out of this context, it requires a burst of fantasy to conjure images of the desert and the mud-brick buildings that surrounded this significant cultic center 3,000 years ago. In our collective conscience in the West, the name Luxor, like that of King Tut or Karnak, is associated with the exotic and supernatural elements of ancient Egypt. Dedicated to the god Amun, Muut (his consort), and Khonsu (his son), it is an imposing complex of structures built on a vast scale, one to rival Karnak Temple in parts, and also enveloped in its own unique and varied religious mysteries.

Architecture

UNLIKE KARNAK, its nearest temple neighbor, the entry pylon constructions at Luxor are finished, but the entry gate is now missing, creating a large opening and a deep view into the interior spaces. At Karnak, the better-known site, our eye saw beyond the pylons, into the great court, the hypostyle hall, and to the distant sanctuary. Here, with its unusual plan configuration, our view ends at the skewed threshold to the Colonnade of Amenhotep III, leaving us to wonder at the factors that inspired this non-orthogonal plan.

A good deal of ink has been split over the last 200 years regarding the layout of the complex; in the last century, the Egyptologist Schwaller de Lubicz, for example, proposed a theory suggesting the human body as the artistic reference (Schwaller 1977). It was one attempt to account for the angled relationships of the various large sections making up the complete temple floor plan. Architects and theoreticians during the European Renaissance developed numerous systems of proportions based on the human figure, which they applied to artistic works, including architecture, so Egyptian artists may have devised a similar approach to their buildings. The theories to account for the eccentricities of this plan geometry suggest the temple layout and its parts could be a metaphor for sections of the human body: the two rectangular entry pylons are the feet; the angle of the colonnade relative to the entry court is the natural, slight bend of the human knee; and the remaining elements correspond to the rest of the body, extending straight up to the sanctuary (the head)—provocative theories that, however, at this time, lack scholarly verification.

At the entry façade of the temple complex, the two original seated statues of Ramesses II remain and flank the opening to the first court, but of the four standing statues once adorning the entry, only one is still in place. In antiquity, the symmetrical balance was reinforced by two obelisks set on each side of the approach. Of the

Court of Ramesses II / Luxor

Statues of Ramesses II / Luxor

two, only one obelisk remains, a typically tapered pyramidal shape, supported on a stone base, here adorned with sculpted baboon monkeys. The other obelisk is now at the center of the Place de la Concorde in Paris, a gift from the ruler of Ottoman Egypt.

In a typical display of self-aggrandizement, the pylons portray Ramesses II in various scenes based on his feats at the Battle of Kadesh and his interaction with deities, but much of the sculpture is severely eroded and nearly indecipherable. Over time, the entrance gate connecting the two majestic pylons was removed or deteriorated and is now virtually gone.

The majority of Egypt's temple plan layouts are orthogonal with a straight linear approach from entry to sanctuary space; Luxor's layout consists of an entrance section that is an oblique parallelogram rotated off center, requiring an angled shift to adjust movement and align with the remainder of the temple structures beyond.

Passing between the massive pylons takes visitors into the Court of Ramesses II, a four-sided space in double columned, peristyle design, once partially roofed, with standing statues of the pharaoh remaining between some of the columns. Awkwardly incorporated into the dominant grid of large, smooth-faced columns with bud capitals is an open, one-story kiosk, placed against the western pylon, whose column shafts, with their vertical, bulged fluting, abstractly refer to bundled papyrus reeds. A transported cult effigy visiting from another temple—Karnak, for example—would have used this spiritually secure place for stopping.

As noted, the geometry of the entry court is non-orthogonal. In addition, the space is askew relative to the rest of the temple and slightly off center, so there is no direct, straight axial progression from the entry pylons to the sanctuary, as at Karnak.

On the east façade of the court is another anomaly to challenge the mind and the eye: the extraordinary insertion of an 11th-century mosque (Abu el-Haggag) set into the original temple fabric, and partly integrated with the eastern pylon and remaining columns. The main floor level starts about thirty feet above the court paving, an impressive indication of the amount of alluvium and dirt that washed over the temple for 1,500 years, now excavated to reveal the full remainder of the ruin, but retaining the mosque.

All this makes for an uncommon introduction, further dramatized by the vista of an allée of imposing, paired columns (seven pairs, seventy feet tall) that makes up the majestic Colonnade of Amenhotep III. Viewed from the Court of Ramesses II, this massive colonnade seems to angle acutely, recalling a still photo of a spectacular train derailment, blocking the vista and leaving the viewer uncertain about what lies beyond and why the plan shifted so dramatically.

This colonnade is a transitional space. By advancing to its threshold and aligning oneself with its center, forward movement is on axis with the sanctuary beyond. Entering it, visitors again move between flanking, seated statues of Ramesses II and continue through a massive corridor with unenclosed lateral spaces.

Next, there is the Sun Court of Amenhotep III whose plan area, at 185 feet by 150 feet, is huge. The court is graced with richly articulated, massed groupings of peristyle columns on three sides, again in double rows. Here, the design of the column shafts and capitals also makes a reference to papyrus reeds with their

Court of Amenhotep III: Columns / Luxor

vertical, bulged fluting, and, at five stories in height, the effect is imposing and dignified.

Originally painted green as a reference to the papyrus plant, the columns are now faded down to the stone surface. Despite the floral inspiration, the effect of each column now is a dazzling approximation of a precise, machine fabricated, mechanistic tool spinning on a circular base. This is convincingly rendered in stonework that is sharp, hard-edged, and exact in execution, a description that also applies to the abacus block above the capital and to the architrave, which connects all the columns. These are among the most beautifully fashioned elements that have survived from Egyptian antiquity.

The court columns have been convincingly integrated with those of the contiguous hypostyle hall, a semi-open structural grid of thirty-two columns, or four rows of eight, filling the transition to the functional section of the temple. In this area, we find numerous rooms and chambers once used for worship, storage, and administration, including the sanctuary, nearly centered in the plan of this wing. Also present in this area of the temple is a repeat of freestanding columns with the papyrus reference, but here they are not as tall as those in the previous court.

Luxor's walls bear the traces and iconographic imprints of numerous dynasties and invaders (including the Greeks, Romans, and Alexander the Great), and the spaces in this temple have served various religious functions, depending on the superior strength and the beliefs of those in power. For example, a Christian church set within this former pagan, polytheistic worship site once occupied the hypostyle hall, and the structure's fabric speaks of numerous ancient beliefs and devotions, charmed with the images and symbols of various faiths. But the presence of the old Egyptian gods and the mysteries of Luxor are still visible in every corner of the complex.

At night, Luxor Temple, like all the significant tourist destinations in Egypt, is ablaze with ground-mounted light fixtures. Each column and statue seem to have risen from an inferno and is now at rest, with milling travelers silhouetted against the light and hieroglyphics in deep shadow. The sensation is like walking through a wonderland of varied spaces with the perimeter of each one on fire, a visually bizarre and near hallucinatory experience that will linger in the memory of every night visitor as images of a revered king and the once-worshiped gods of Luxor.

Ramesses II / Luxor

Temple Entrance Façade / Luxor

Valley of the Kings

DAY 6

DEPARTING FROM KARNAK crossing the Nile and driving through farmland (some farmers still using the ox for cultivation) and featureless desert terrain, we arrive at the site of one of the 20th century's greatest discoveries: the tomb field containing the burial chamber of Tut-Ankh-Amun, the boy pharaoh who died at nineteen. For a society devoted to the eternal privacy of a pharaoh's resting place, this burial site of four small rooms and its king's treasures are now among the most recognizable artifacts of all time, and his peace has been disturbed by throngs of thousands exploring this rocky hollow for nearly 100 years.

KV 62 Signage / Valley of the Kings

LOCATED ON THE NILE'S WEST BANK, directly across the mountain ridge that forms the backdrop to the Mortuary Temple of Queen Hatshepsut, the Valley of the Kings is the setting for the royal necropolis of the New Kingdom.

In a vain attempt to stop the looting of pharaonic burial chambers, this remote site was chosen as the new royal tomb field beginning with Pharaoh Tuthmosis I (KV 20), and it remained the royal necropolis for 500 years.

Set in the limestone valley or "wadi" created by eons of water run-off, the site is a massive stone trough of blistering heat and glare, devoid of vegetation and with little shade. To date, within this rocky terrain, sixty-three numbered subterranean tombs have been discovered, the most famous being KV 62.

As very visible public monuments to a pharaoh's life and reign, the pyramid tombs are among the largest structures of all time. This building type was eventually abandoned for the anonymity of subterranean, unmarked tombs set in an indistinctive terrain. Instead of burial in man-made mountains, pharaohs returned to the body of mother earth in the mass and density of a natural cliff formation, appropriately located on the west side of the Nile, where Hathor welcomed Amun-Ra, the sun god, at the dying of each day.

Al-Qurn Summit / Valley of the Kings

Introduction

FROM THE DROP-OFF POINT, one walks up a paved incline mixing with hundreds of tourists heading out into the rugged terrain in search of a specific tomb. Each tomb is listed with an individual KV number, with the designation as an abbreviation for K[ings'] V[alley].

At the periphery, laborers are at work excavating the site in the scorching, heavy heat of midday. To a passenger on one of the area's numerous balloon tours, the scene from above must resemble a massive ant hill, with people swarming over rocky contours and darting in and out of narrow slit openings in the ground.

The summit, known as Al-Qurn, where the two cliff ridges meet, is a natural formation that resembles a blunted pyramid shape, or as one historian has noted, "From the valley, the mound is nippled and strongly resembles the breast of Hathor herself" (Scully 1991, 30). As the goddess of birth, death, and cosmic renewal, she encompassed the full span of life's journey in this world and beyond to the afterlife. It forms a natural crown to the whole burial site.

Architecture

A MAP OF THE VALLEY, which includes all the subterranean tombs and chambers located to date, illustrates a seemingly strewn array of corridors and multichamber excavations, with some overlapping in plan but not intersecting vertically. There is evidence, however, that in the original process of excavation, several tomb floor plans were altered due to conflicts with existing chambers or their access corridors. A number of tombs are multileveled and some are quite large in area and extensive in length (one tomb is over 120 rooms), continuing the practice of opulent and image-rich space making for the resting place of their king and pharaoh.

Entrance to Tomb of Pharaoh Tuthmosis III / Valley of the Kings

The practice of cutting and transporting cyclopean, stone blocks to be erected as pyramids, the largest 450 feet in height, had been replaced here with the primeval drive to return to earth "caves" under the protection of the goddess Hathor. To assist the soul in the transition from life to the death state and after, the rock walls were plastered and decorated by artists and scribes living in nearby Deir el-Medina with scenes of daily, normative life (at least for a pharaoh) and eternal, supernatural existence. Many of these narrative paintings are enthralling with a brilliant display of color and implied movement, profusely covering every inch of every surface, including ceilings. Appropriately, the nocturnal journey through the underworld by the god Amun-Ra is a pervasive theme in these burial illustrations.

Ultimately, the measures taken to sustain the tombs in an inviolate condition failed (even the Tomb of Tuthmosis III (KV 34) located 100 feet above the ground and now accessible only by an exterior stair, was robbed of its riches), and all tombs, save one, were robbed of their artifacts, prompting speculation on the riches that might have been buried with pharaohs of longer and more important reigns than that of King Tut-ankh-amun.

There may yet be a myriad of unknown chambers sealed and hidden about the landscape, and the search for other tombs or relics goes on.

KV 62

ON THE DAY OF OUR VISIT, we find ourselves in an environment of bleached out, chalk-colored rock and sand in search of KV 62. Moving from the densely heated air and the glare of midday, we step into the shaded entrance and then across the threshold into the below-grade corridor of KV 62, a step that brings on a flash of momentary anticipation at entering one of the most famous tombs of all time, the resting place for the soul of the best known (although not the most significant) of Egypt's pharaohs. It is a stark transition from the radiant valley down into the mysterious, dream-like surrealism of the occult that occupies the chambers of King Tut's tomb.

The sole resident of KV 62 for 3,000 years, the pharaoh depicted in his famous funerary mask of gold and gems (having, as some have expressed it, the looks of a teen idol), despite spells and curses to guard his solitude, became a 20th-century global sensation, possibly the most recognized face from the ancient world.

Pharaoh Tut-ankh-amun (translated as "living image of Amun"), a minor figure with a nine-year reign who died young at nineteen, commands a renown based almost entirely on the artifacts found in his burial chambers. Despite the warnings found on his tomb ("Death will come on swift wings to him that disturbs the sleep of the Pharaoh.") and the measures taken to ensure his eternal anonymity and peace, it remains, understandably, the most frequently visited site in the Valley of the Kings.

A flight of steps takes us down to an inclined plane that leads to Howard Carter's discovery of 1922, a space reverberating with his now famous remark when asked if he could see anything of interest through a small exploratory opening in the tomb wall: "Yes, I see wonderful things." His explorations were to yield an argosy of riches: priceless objects piled high with furniture, statues, food, sarcophagi, and other equipment necessary to exist in the afterlife. In the nearly 100 years since his discovery, the amount and the quality of the artifacts unearthed here have never been equaled or surpassed.

Tut-ankh-amun's burial place is relatively small, comprising a set of steps, an inclined corridor and four sealed rooms: antechamber, annex, treasury, and burial chamber. Unlike numerous examples in the Valley of the Kings where the connecting corridors are covered with highly colored murals full of figures and gods, the walls of the corridor to the pharaoh's tomb are unadorned and left plain, possibly an indication that Tut's burial may have been a hasty undertaking following his premature death. This lack of decorative wall treatment applies to all the rooms, except for Tut-ankh-amun's burial chamber.

The Spaces:

Antechamber: First room, once containing tables, chests, baskets, small chariots, and two statues flanking the entrance to the burial chamber

Annex: Sealed room, furniture once piled high

Treasury: A space with an opening to the burial chamber, at one time featuring a shrine, numerous chests, small boat models, and miscellaneous items

Burial Chamber: Tut-ankh-amun's coffin room

THE BURIAL CHAMBER is a small space (approximately twenty-one feet by twelve feet), which at one time was substantially filled with a massive burial shrine in the center, nearly extending to the walls. This royal shrine consisted of nine nested containers with the mummified pharaoh's coffin in the first container. The outer box had double doors to access six additional boxes, three of which were gold-covered, "body"-shaped sarcophagi.

In the burial chamber, all walls are completely painted with the figures depicting gods, goddesses, animals, and scenes illustrating the pharaoh's life and afterlife. The south wall, of particular interest, illustrates a scene showing the king flanked by two deities: Anubis, the black, jackal-headed god of mummification, and Hathor, the goddess of renewal. Each is holding the ankh, the cross-shaped symbol of life, looped at the upper vertical, with Hathor also holding an additional ankh to the pharaoh's lips in the "opening of the mouth" ceremony, which allowed the pharaoh to breathe and speak, reanimating the king, now suspended in the realm of the dead.

This vital symbol, held by the gods in this scene and in many other depictions we would encounter on our trip, more than any other piece of iconography, appeared to represent the essence of Egyptian fantasy and the culture's most potent tool for extending life after death.

Entrance to KV 62 / Valley of the Kings

We may assume that the burial chambers hollowed out in the Valley of the Kings, had they remained inviolate, would have entombed the greatest accumulation of treasures and the most concentrated spiritual field in all of ancient Egypt and, conceivably, the ancient world at that time: a royal necropolis laden with invaluable riches; hundreds of chambers gracefully adorned with paintings and carvings; and a skewed, supernatural matrix of deified kings. Standing in Pharaoh Tut's burial chamber, mentally imposing his magnificent mask of gold and lapis lazuli on the leathery face of his mummy, gave a suggestion of the full measure of splendor once accumulated within the jagged terrain of this remote, dry, and secluded valley.

Mortuary Temple of Hatshepsut

DAY 7

AS AN ARCHITECT, my initial reaction to photos of Hatshepsut's Mortuary Temple was one of astonishment: Displayed was a structure constructed 3,500 years ago with elements abstractly reminiscent of examples from late 20th-century modern architectural design. This temple's aesthetic consists of straight lines, simple structural elements, and openings that are large and rectangular in shape—its pronounced horizontality set against a rugged backdrop of uneven, fissured cliffs of shale and limestone. It makes no pretense of organic integration with the site: It is a radical, brilliantly conceived departure from the pylon-fronted temples of Karnak and Philae, expressed as what may be considered an anomalous masterwork of Egyptian architecture.

UNDER A BRILLIANT SUN, we stand on the temple's upper terrace before one of the massive statues of the bearded Queen Hatshepsut in Osiriform pose. With a sense of authority, she looks beyond us and the crowds, down to the river Nile and beyond to the Theban landscape and the city of Karnak. Once there existed a phalanx of twenty-six widely spaced Hatshepsut statues—one at each pier face—across this expansive façade (approximately 200 feet in length), but presently, there are only six remaining, leaving a mere remnant of what must have been a powerful display of authority.

Compared to the fleshy and blunted facial contours of the Great Sphinx or Ramesses II, her features are unmistakably feminine in the delicacy of the nose and brow. Upon the death of her father, Tuthmosis I, she assumed the throne, and her reign was notable for its social stability, prosperity, and for the significant quantity of building projects, including monumental temple

Hatshepsut Pier Statue / Mortuary Temple of Hatshepsut

Mortuary Temple of Hatshepsut

Horus Statue at Ramp / Mortuary Temple of Hatshepsut

In the tomb of Queen Hatshepsut ... the pyramid disappeared completely and the tomb was cut deep into the cliff itself. Hatshepsut would seem to have positioned herself as closely as she could to the magical shape of the cliff. Before her chamber, she laid out broad garden parterres,... probably planted thick with trees.

—Scully (1991, 30)

Interior Colonnade / Mortuary Temple of Hatshepsut

Façade Colonnade / Mortuary Temple of Hatshepsut

buildings undertaken during her reign; she is often referred to as one of the first great women in Western history.

As the eye of Amun-Ra climbs into a cloudless azure sky, the entire landscape is resplendent with light and alive with the movement of travelers, walking about the temple, climbing up and down the site on its wide ramps, and stepping in and out of thin slivers of shade.

The wide, connecting ramps, which are a striking architectural feature, dominate the approach, and, in keeping with the Egyptian ritual of procession, create the same axial focus on the sanctuary space of the cult god positioned just off the upper terrace. Movement from the Nile to the mortuary temple would have been enhanced by a transitional rise in elevation at each terrace, the cavalcade proceeding both horizontally forward and vertically upward, finally breaching the mountain face and penetrating deeply into the desert cliff. Here the deity would reside until its return to Karnak.

Rituals in Antiquity

IN ANTIQUITY, THE CELEBRATION of the "Beautiful Festival of the Valley" publicly recognized Hathor, the cow goddess, as the patron deity of birth, death, and cosmic renewal. In this ceremony, the cult figure of Amun was carried from temple to river to mountain, points of religious meaning and importance, as the deity effigy was transported from Karnak Temple to where Hathor was imagined to dwell, across the Nile, in the hills west of Thebes.

On that day, the procession, including the Amun boat shrine, left the temple at Karnak, crossed the Nile and visited the first structure on its Hathor pilgrimage, Hatshepsut's Valley Temple, on the opposite river bank. From there, the assembly advanced by walled causeway to the second stop, the Barque Shrine, where the effigy would rest. Next, the procession moved west at ground level through the expansive, walled lower terrace/first court, the path defined by a sphinx-lined allée with flanking exotic gardens and symmetrically placed pools of water, until it reached the first of the wide ramps. Advancing in the ascent, the procession would arrive at the middle terrace/second court, a wide plateau, with another sphinx allée defining the way. Finally, the cortege moved up the last ramp, and arrived at the upper terrace/third court, passing between the phalanxed statues of the Osiriform Hatshepsut, arriving at the open court directly in front of the Amun chamber entrance. In the sanctuary chamber, the deity would be securely installed and shielded deep within the living rock of the mountain and, as the faithful believed, within the body of Hathor.

Architecture

THE ARCHITECTURE OF THE TEMPLE is magnificent in the breadth of its façade and impressively sculpted in the depths of its shadows. A range of cliffs separating the site from the Valley of the Kings creates a dramatic, irregular, and fissured backdrop to the low horizontality of sharp-edged colonnades that constitute the major pieces of the temple façade. Aesthetically, it represents an original and dramatic break with the architectural language of the great Egyptian pylon-fronted temples and pointed pyramids of the past.

The terrace-court projections extend out into the desert landscape as tiers, mounting to a height of over ninety feet at the third court, and every level is open to the sky; each elevational change is delineated with a colonnade of piers, with columns and fascia marking the transition to another tier.

Today, the architectural style might be labeled "antique modern" for the essential characteristics of its geometrical abstraction. Of the three limestone façades, the first two are bisected by wide ramps at the center, and each consists of colonnades of simple

Interior Colonnade / Mortuary Temple of Hatshepsut

square-edged bays of trabeated (post and lintel) construction. At the uppermost tier, the colonnade also stretches for the entire length of the façade, interrupted only by the entrance opening to the third court, once flanked by the full complement of Hatshepsut statues.

The ruins of the architecturally influential temples of Mentuhotep II and Tuthmosis III, and the Chapel of Hathor, are on the left (to the west) as visitors ascend the ramps. A portion of the Hathor Chapel remains or has been reinstated, but the walls and superstructure of the temples are now completely missing, leaving only the foundation platform. They are, however, surpassed by the grandeur and originality exhibited in the wide expanse of the Mortuary Temple of Hatshepsut, devised by her architect, Senenmut.

Interestingly, many of the columns here may be broadly described as Grecian influenced: pillars that are faceted in plan with a simple block abacus capital and a minimal, round base. They occur behind each of the rectangular façade piers and at the once fully colonnaded third court.

This atypical treatment, spare and geometric, may also reflect a knowledge of Minoan architecture and is a considerable contrast to the prevalent Egyptian column type characterized by luxuriant, vegetal-inspired capitals and hieroglyphic markings on the shaft or by the highly detailed Hathor-headed column tops on the ruins of the adjacent temple.

At the third court, before the entrance to the Sanctuary of Amun, what appears to be a kiosk with "Egyptian"-style columns is now mostly in ruin. The colonnade here, once three columns deep, is nearly gone, revealing the perimeter walls of the precinct. Door openings on the north and south walls of the court once provided access to the flanking Chapel of the Royal Cult or the Chapel of the Solar Cult. The west elevation of the upper court is punctuated with alternating tall and short niches; statues would have occupied the taller niches, creating an interesting point/counterpoint architectural treatment.

The cult effigy's journey ended with its positioning in a chamber cut sixty feet into the mountain body. Since this mortuary temple lacks supporting ancillary spaces, it is presumed that this was a temporary residence of the god to be used only during ceremonies and then returned to Thebes.

Set against the sheer face and rugged backdrop of the West Bank's Theban cliffs, Hatshepsut's Mortuary Temple seems surprisingly contemporary and aesthetically relevant, with its rational, square-edged geometry stepping out into the desert plain to accommodate, in contrast, the mystical superstitions of cultic ceremony and ritual taking place around and within its walls.

Unlike the accepted styles applied to the majority of Egyptian structures of canted walls and towering pylons, it does not appear to have exerted any significant aesthetic influence on later generations of temple builders, making the complex unequaled and singular.

Third Court / Mortuary Temple of Hatshepsut

Kiosk Detail / Mortuary Temple of Hatshepsut

Third Court: Kiosk and Entrance / Mortuary Temple of Hatshepsut

Kom Ombo

DAY 8

FROM OUR ELEVATED BOAT DECK, we descend on Kom Ombo much as the gods, Horus the Elder and Sobek, approached their temple: the falcon in flight and the crocodile skimming the surface of the Nile. Set on elevated ground within a few hundred feet of the river, the superstructure of the rare dual temple at Kom Ombo emerges majestically above the tree line, its mirrored image shimmering in shallow undulations on the waters of the river's surface. Seen from this vantage point as we near the dock, the hulking stone mass, impressively modeled in deep shadow, gives the impression of a magnificent, god-sized brow rising from this perennially dust-covered terrain to survey the latest legion of visitors, as it has for over 2,000 years.

AS A TWO-DEITY TEMPLE, one might expect Kom Ombo to be twice the size of a standard temple, but such is not the case—the building is simply bisected down the center, each half being the mirror image of the other. In this polytheistic religion, this juxtaposition was apparently acceptable, and the structure has been designed around this accommodation.

Kom Ombo is atypical in several other respects: one conjectural reconstruction shows the Nile as situated adjacent to the outer walls of the complex, precluding pedestrian access directly on axis with the sanctuary chamber. If correct, the approach was from the north, parallel to the Nile, entering through the Gate of Ptolemy XII, which is located on the eastern face of the perimeter masonry wall.

Today, an impressively wide set of modern stairs links the dock level with the temple entrance, a very different perspective from that seen by a Kom Ombian in 40 BC. On the slow ascent from

Entrance Court / Kom Ombo

Entrance Court + Gate of Ptolemy XII / Kom Ombo

Entrance Façade / Kom Ombo

the river's edge, the perceived "brow" and "face" are transfigured and expand into the spectacular ruins of the temple façade featuring twin portals, one for each deity.

Architecture

ARRIVING AT THE TOP OF THE ENTRY STAIR, the temple façade is directly before us—to the right are the remains of the Gate of Ptolemy XII, to the left stand the remains of the mammisi, and immediately before us are the vestiges of the columns that defined the Court of Augustus. The massive, fractured structure that represents part of the pronaos (vestibule) and hypostyle hall is, to a great extent, what remains of the original temple construction. Begun in the 2nd century BC by Ptolemy VI Philometor, it took 150 years and several phases to complete. In ancient times, this once-compact sacred precinct, enclosed by a typical high mud brick wall with an undulating parapet, included this rare two-deity temple, a mammisi, an additional deity chapel (Hathor), a basin for keeping live crocodiles, a nilometer to measure river height, storage buildings, and living quarters. Here, the supernatural spirit of Horus commanded the sky while Sobek inhabited the waters of the Nile.

In terms of architectural formality, a pharaoh or priest entered from the east, moving parallel to the Nile through the substantial Ptolemy gate and into a narrow transitional space within the temple's outer enclosure wall. This relatively narrow, unroofed space was once defined by the Ptolemy gate (significantly gone), the mammisi (only floor and small wall areas remain), and the outer enclosure wall (significantly missing). At this point, the procession turned north to enter the temple through the Courtyard of Augustus.

In this twin-deity arrangement, Horus the Elder, the falcon-headed god associated with the sun and the sky, occupied the western half of the temple and Sobek, the crocodile-headed god associated with fertility and ferocity, occupied the eastern half. The Courtyard of Augustus provided open space for gathering directly before the twin entrances with a columned U-shaped portico (sixteen columns, total, on three sides). It was a relatively small and intimate space for public ceremony, with a ritual altar located in the middle, positioned on center with the temple façade. Today, there is no sense of enclosure, but the remaining column stubs mark the footprint of the original terrace and give a sense of its measurements.

Architecturally, the temple layout is remarkable for positioning a substantial stone pier and column at the center of the entry façade. The traditional plan layout is to center an open bay (the space between two columns) on the temple façade, thus allowing axial movement between columns at the center of the façade. At Kom Ombo, each god has a dedicated entrance and a dedicated sanctuary, so the façade, although still symmetrical, is functionally split, with the processional movement to a particular cult deity occurring on either side of the massive stone pier in the center. With the temple's dual occupation, equal cultic functions required a plan mirrored along the center of the building; consequently, there is a shared, symmetrical vestibule and hypostyle hall, but individual ante chambers, rooms for worship, and storage for each god.

The temple façade features typical Ptolemaic components: knee walls fill the space between columns and run across the breadth of the elevation. Each is integrated with a pair of columns (three of the original five majestic façade columns remain), whose shafts rise up and blossom into a brilliant array of vegetal-inspired capitals. This is the "face" of Kom Ombo, the image most reproduced and known to the Nile traveler.

A superstructure of stone lintels, capped by a massive frieze with an impressive cavetto profile makes the transition from building to sky. Taking the path to the sanctuary, ten equally impressive

West Elevation / Kom Ombo

View to Hypostyle Hall / Kom Ombo

West Elevation / Kom Ombo

columns support the roof of the vestibule with the wall between it and the hypostyle hall still partially intact. As we move beyond the hall, a few columns, lintels, and partial walls have survived, conveying the sense of double openings in the approach to each deity sanctuary, but then the building suddenly thins down into a few wall remnants and beams.

Another site construction we found architecturally fascinating (included in many temple complexes) was the prominently featured nilometer. At Kom Ombo, it is a cylinder-shaped, stone-lined shaft, open to the sky, that descends to the level of the Nile. The meter is a masonry cylinder, appearing very much like a conventional well but with stone steps descending to river level, a location that allowed the temple priests to periodically measure water levels, thus helping to predict future flow rates (the extent of flooding) and gauge its effect on a season's harvest, a crucial estimation in this predominately agrarian culture.

We visited the site near sunset, and when night fell the temple came alive with the ground-mounted illumination that is typical at these monuments. Gone are the preternatural mysteries of darkened chambers for cultic ritual so essential to invoking the spirit of Horus and Sobek, but in their place, the contrivance of artificial lighting imparts a surreal glow that creates its own kind of fantasy effect: with the bas-reliefs of gods and royalty etched out in a luminance set against the night sky and, on this particular evening, a full moon.

Hypostyle Hall / Kom Ombo

Nilometer / Kom Ombo

Edfu

DAY 9

I FIRST ENCOUNTERED THE MYTHIC TALE of Horus and his uncle Seth in the novel *Ancient Evenings* by the American writer Norman Mailer. Mailer's depiction of their explosive power struggle is a wild, febrile account based on the fantasy tales once spun by ancient Egyptian mythmakers, in this case hypercharged with extraordinary violence. At Edfu, Horus's association with this temple is acknowledged by large statues of Horus flanking the entrances; and it is conceivable that many versions of this story were acted out within the temple, its courts, and on the sacred lake, now buried beneath contemporary Edfu.

The city itself is a typical, modern-day Egyptian urban landscape, consisting of blocks of pale-colored, low-rise buildings connected by dusty streets with merchants selling their wares in ground floor shops. In the center sits one of Egypt's best-preserved temples.

THE DRAMA that chronicled the extended power struggle between Horus and his uncle Seth is a bizarre narrative of tumultuous, protracted physical conflicts whose details and participants have changed over time and locale. In an early example of deicide, as told, Seth kills his brother, King Osiris, dismembers the body, and scatters the parts around Egypt and even, in some versions of the tale, into areas of the Mediterranean Basin, allowing Seth to assume the crown. The various body pieces of Osiris are eventually located and reassembled by his sister, Isis (also his queen in some tales). In this state, Osiris lives long enough to impregnate her and father a future heir (Horus) before the former king must descend to the Duat (underworld) to become the ruler of that dark domain. At maturity, Horus engages in furious

Horus Statue / Edfu

Entrance Panorama / Edfu

struggles with Seth in a contest to gain or retain the throne. Seth is eventually vanquished, and, as the rightful heir of Osiris, Horus finally assumes his position as king. As an allegorical tale, Horus's triumph established a validation for the transference of rule through regal lineage and served as an example of the struggle for royal power in the real world.

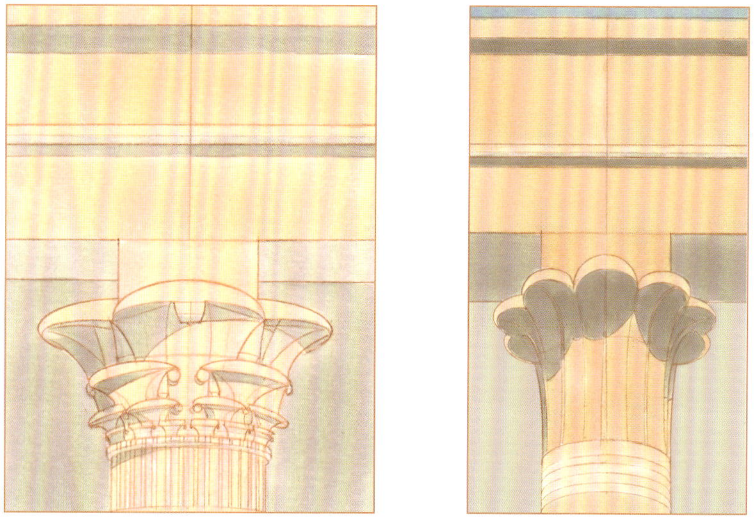

Column Capitals / Edfu

Mammisi / Edfu

Forecourt + Temple Entrance Façade / Edfu

Architecture

EDFU'S GREATEST ATTRACTION is the temple dedicated to the falcon-headed deity, Horus. Started under Ptolemy III in 237 BC and completed by Ptolemy XII Neo Dionysus in 57 BC, it is roughly contemporary and architecturally similar to the temple at Philae and is well preserved after being substantially buried for hundreds of years.

Driving through the city, we turn onto Al Mabed Road and see the rear and west elevations of the temple as we approach the parking area. The view as we arrive at the site is not encouraging: parked buses idling on a sea of tarmac; to the east, a long, open shelter made of simple metal pipe construction, divided into bays and covered in light thatch, used by horse-drawn taxis or "calesh." Opposite that is a long, one-story, nondescript structure, recently built for vendors, with an opening in the middle leading to an angled paved walk to the temple.

This is another site where access to the complex requires a fairly lengthy trek to the temple itself. En route, we pass between mud brick ruins of other ancient constructions before gaining a full view of the mammisi with the temple pylons in the background. Unlike temples such as Karnak and Luxor, Edfu is located on the west side of the Nile, oriented on an axial approach running north/south through the center of the temple sanctuary.

This once expansive sacred precinct is now wedged into a patch of residual space between mud brick ruins and the city of Edfu (Horus would not be pleased). In the midst of this dry townscape, the temple, massive and monolithic, resembles a great vessel that appears to have run aground, stranded on land once the waters have receded.

Once past the ancient excavations, we have a view, scanning from east to west, of the city of Edfu, the temple entry pylons, and the ruins of the mammisi in the foreground. From archaeological evidence, it appears that Edfu lacked the strict, symmetrical

View from Entry Portal to Temple / Edfu

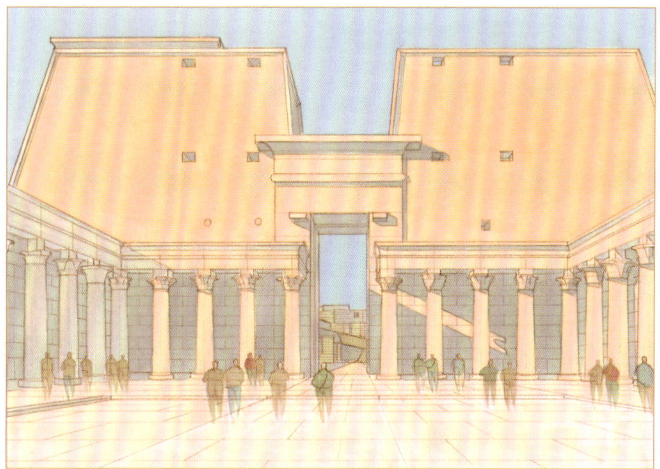

View from Temple to Pylons / Edfu

Temple Façade Detail / Edfu

approach to the sanctuary from the entry point. Instead, the path is somewhat askew relative to the pylon gate.

In general, the Temple of Horus itself stands as one of the best-preserved examples of this building type in Egypt, with all major parts, except for the mammisi and its contiguous open court walls, in excellent condition. Of the temples we visited, it was the only one to retain its enclosure wall: the perimeter construction extending from the outer ends of the entry pylons to approximately fifteen feet beyond the sanctuary block.

Moving on, we arrive at an axial position of what remains of the former precinct gate, and the great entry pylons present themselves in full elevation. Even now, devoid of painted color, obelisks, and flanking colossi at the entry façade, they are magnificent in scale and solidity, looming over the entire view as we near the entrance. Here is a design following the accepted Ptolemaic layout: a stately entry portal (50 feet high) is merged with and flanked by massive pylons (115 feet high). Consistent with similar temples, the pylon façades are gigantic "billboards" of propaganda, both political and religious. Displayed in carvings approximately twenty feet high are Horus and Ptolemy engaging in battle on either side of the entry gate with miscellaneous scenes of rituals in rows above. Imposing in stature and towering in elevation, the entrance portal is massive and thick, embellished with a radiant sun disc at the lintel and topped with a deep cavetto molding curving out into space. The analogy here is the sun radiating between the pylons as "mountains," creating a reference to nature and the sun god, Amun-Ra. Black-granite statues of Horus as a falcon, one on each side of the gate entrance, symbolically mark the transition to the occult world, moving toward the sanctuary.

One passes between the paired pylons flanking the entrance portal into a vast court articulated on three sides with a colonnade of thirty-two massive columns in a peristyle arrangement. The temple enclosure wall defines the extent of the court space. Unlike Classical Greek or Roman architecture where all column capitals are normally identical within an individual structure, the capitals here and at many other Egyptian sites are elaborate, highly decorative, quasi-floral designs, in a variety of styles within a single building. This makes for a less classical or "pure" embellishment; however, the Egyptians were not aspiring to classicism but to an exotic exaggeration of their flora's natural features.

This temple forecourt is a special response to a special function. Open to the sky, it is a space both grand and intimate. From the approach, the entry pylons dominate the architecture and seem to stand alone as geometric mountain shapes in a desert landscape, but when viewed from the interior court, the pylons, now integrated with the colonnade (also massive), take on a different aspect with two parallel colonnades extending from the pylons to the temple, stopping just short of the hypostyle hall façade. This is somewhat like the figure of the Giza Sphinx: a tall solid mass with two "arms" extending from its body. The center of the court was once occupied by a ceremonial altar, leaving ample space for spectators on various festival days.

The temple layout and architectural treatment follow the standard design models of this period. At the front entrance, three columns, integrated with low screen walls, flank each side of a typical entry portal with the lintel broken at the head (top). These six columns are centered in a façade of battered end walls, all crowned with a deep cavetto fascia molding at the roof line. Black-granite statues of Horus flank the entrance and frame the approach, repeating the paired statues at the entrance and reinforcing the symmetry.

We enter the temple: the first hypostyle hall with its twelve giant, densely spaced columns leads to a smaller, second hypostyle hall, also tightly packed with twelve columns. Each column, with its leafy capital, establishes a reference to the natural world immediately outside the deity chamber, thus making a connection to the falcon's habitat.

Proceeding deeper, we arrive at the sanctuary, a narrow, tall

Temple Enclosure Wall / Edfu

space, once the residence of the cult figure, still equipped with altar and pedestal for the deity barque. The sanctuary is surrounded by rooms and chambers, proportionately very tall, covered with carvings of mythological incident and pharaonic interaction with the gods. In typical layout, an internal stair provides access to the roof.

We stood in these spaces and tried to imagine the rituals of long ago and the nature of the architecture here. Did the room shape and size refer to some cosmic proportion, or was it based on the perceived grandeur required for the proper authority of a god?

In addition, the temple building is secured with an enclosure wall that stretches from the entry façade of the temple to fifteen feet beyond the rear of the building that creates a U-shaped passage open to the sky. Battered, windowless stone walls rise on each side of this narrow space, which is only fifteen feet wide at its base. Standing in this perimeter zone, looking south, the enclosure wall extends past the mass of the hypostyle hall, creating a dynamic relationship of angled planes and stark physicality and weight. It is a passage without an active function: a vacant, pharaoh-formed valley of stone, powerful in its space-making.

Mythic recreations, such as the transformation of Horus and Seth into hippopotami (Isis, as motherly protector, attempts to harpoon Seth) were once conducted on the sacred lake located to the east of the temple and now buried under present day Edfu.

With Edfu, we are near the end of the Egyptian dynastic period, once politically extended by Roman occupation; it is the last exhalation of the ancients in Egypt. As the denouement of a particular civilization's history of architecture, it is a fitting conclusion to a remarkable 2,000 years of building. That history includes some of the greatest structures ever erected, and Edfu, in its remarkable condition, is an impressive artifact of a unique time and place and people

Temple North Façade / Edfu

Temple and Enclosure Wall / Edfu

View to Horus Statue / Edfu

Dendera

DAY 10

Dendera Light

AMONG THE THOUSANDS OF CARVED IMAGES presented to us on our travels, each impressive in its own way, the so-called "Dendera Light" bas-relief captured our imagination unlike any other. To behold this enigmatic carving, it was necessary to literally crawl into the crypt of the temple on hands and knees, where we found ourselves in a long, narrow space with shallow sculptures covering all surfaces except the floor. Even with the superabundance of characters and scenes depicted on this chamber's walls, the Dendera Light stood out as a superb example of pure mythic imagination in the subtle modulations of its stone carvings and the magical characters displayed in this ancient scene.

IN A NARROW, STONE-WALLED CRYPT beneath the late Ptolemaic Temple of Hathor at Dendera, amid dense hieroglyphic wall carvings, is a "tableau" whose ritualistic depiction ranks among the most enigmatic and provocative to have been unearthed from ancient Egypt. Set in the central horizontal section of a three-panel wall division are two nearly symmetrical carvings facing each other. Each depicts what appears to be the birth of a desert serpent as it sinuously extends from the receptacle of a lotus flower, stretching into the center of a transparent, bulbous volume. A stem connects one lotus to a rectangular block, while the other stem disappears at the panel's bottom. Supporting the scene are integrated figures of men and a set of horizontal bars, sprouting arms and hands (a motif not seen every day) that support one bulb.

Temple Façade / Dendera

Entry Gate / Dendera

What creates comment and interest around this particular, odd (to us) scene is the resemblance of the bulge, snake, receptacle, and stem, to a 20th-century tubular light bulb, including its cable and power source. As unusual as this may sound, the parts are all there, and experimenters in the 20th century have built working light fixtures using this simple image. For a peripheral group of thinkers, this infers a knowledge and a use of electric current by the ancient Egyptians. Serious archeology has rejected this interpretation, but there is still a faction that considers this a viable interpretation of what appears to be a working mechanism, of sorts.

Standing before these images in this low and narrow space, there is a temptation to add a layer of modern science over these markings, but mere resemblance is not proof of reality. Whatever it may portray, these unusual figures and the scene depicted must have had meaning for Egyptians 2,000 years ago.

When only considered as image, however, the scene typifies the essence of what might be referred to as the "Egyptian effect": the graphic admixture of humans, animals, and flora into an intoxicating overlap of exotic characters and ritual depictions. Visually knitted together in action or message, they represent an intricate and complex religious tradition, manifested in rites and explained or elaborated in texts and hieroglyphics. This fusion is, I think, the mystical essence of this land of eternal questions.

The Hathor Temple embodies this cultural evolution at its most advanced stage, and the mythographers who conceived of the "Dendera Light," whatever it may represent, showed remarkable imagination in this artistic invention, executed with beauty and conviction.

Entry Gate / Dendera

"Dendera Light" in Temple of Hathor / Dendera

Mammisi Façade Detail / Dendera

Site

FROM ARCHAEOLOGICAL EVIDENCE, the temple complex at Dendera was a site dense with buildings: temples to Hathor and Isis, two mammisi, a sacred lake, mastabas, and numerous ancillary structures all packed rather tightly into the precinct once dedicated to the veneration of the important goddess Hathor.

This remote spot on the Nile served as sacred ground to a number of cultures and religions over thousands of years. Dendera's array of structures are contained within a massively thick, high, mud brick wall, laid in undulating courses, representing the ancient waters of Nun (the god of the primeval ocean) before the creation of the world. Three gates breach this outer wall, with the eastern pylon (the one facing the Nile) as the main entrance, admitting the visitor to a generous open space directly before the temple façade. The original complex, prior to Christian assumption, formed an impressive assembly of buildings and an ideal mechanism for worship that must have pleased the deity.

From our transportation drop-off, it is quite a long walk to the entrance of this large temple precinct, an approach that is flanked by flat grass land with no edifices, so the complex seems somewhat isolated. We near the entrance on axis and stop before the fractured remains of the entry gate; to either side of us are the vestiges of Roman constructions in the form of eight small columns and two wells. We pass through the remains of the massive gate ruin into a large public space, pause before the temple and visually survey the ground: a vista of numerous structures, large and small, most in good but reduced condition.

Temple South Façade / Dendera

Mammisi Façade / Dendera

Sacred Lake / Dendera

Architecture

TODAY, THE HATHOR TEMPLE, one of the best-preserved examples of this building type in Egypt, is a superb example of late Ptolemaic architecture. All other major structures are still extant and a good deal of the perimeter mud brick wall remains, although in ruins.

After entering the complex, we see, to the right, the remains of the Egyptian mammisi, turned ninety degrees from the temple's axis; its design and layout are architecturally similar to other mammisi, such as at Edfu. Adjacent to the mammisi stands the ruin of a Coptic church and directly before us is the temple with a distinctive group of eighteen columns in its entry vestibule; looking beyond, to each side, the vast mud brick enclosure wall built by the Romans encircles the site.

From a distance, the columns and capitals in the temple vestibule are obscured. Here, as we observed in other temples, the open space between columns at the façade have been filled in with wire fabric, presumably to keep insects and birds out, so the rows of impressive Hathor-headed columns in the vestibule space are barely visible until we are quite near.

Inside the vestibule, every inch of every surface is adorned with image-rich hieroglyphics, either painted or in bas-relief, on column, wall, and ceiling. A good deal of the original color is visible, even though muted by time or deliberately damaged by each new religion taking occupancy. As the temple's most distinctive interior feature, each face of the square column capital is decorated with a magnificent sculpted head of Hathor with cow ears (as the cow goddess). The nose and center of each head are severely damaged, defiled by Christians who occupied this precinct at one time, yet even with this mutilation, there is still a remarkable presence in the sculptural quality of the head and hair draped around the face. This room, seen in the filtered light entering between piers, is an enchanting space: Eighteen

Sacred Lake / Dendera

closely centered columns richly carved with hieroglyphics define the room vertically, so the expression is akin to moving through a dense forest. The effect is sheltering and protective, and one feels surrounded by extraordinary creatures with supernatural powers, seemingly sprung from nature.

One other detail of the pronaos is distinctive: The wall dividing the vestibule from the adjacent hypostyle hall features a temple-like façade, complete with battered, sloping half-round torus moldings at each end, a short plinth at the floor and a great curving cavetto fascia near the ceiling. This wall is a delightful and unexpected architectural treatment that adds an element of superb detail to an already special environment.

Temple of Hathor
Lion Spout / Dendera

Rooftop Kiosk Detail / Dendera

Once past the pronaos and the hypostyle hall, the interior is a typical series of chambers once used for storage, wardrobe, offerings, and other related functions required to administer the daily rituals to the goddess, all grouped around the sanctuary space centered within the main worship block.

The chambers themselves, tall volumes of space, animated with bas-relief wall hieroglyphics, are now, of course, empty. So we feel this as an experience of pure, sheltering space, now redundant and without function, but beautiful in its proportions and ornament. Enhancing that dimension is the oblique wash of sunlight or up-lighting on the wall carvings, casting them into relief and illuminating millennia-old narratives. The ambiance is primordial, like peering through a window into a foreign culture, existing outside of familiar reference or verification.

Another interior space within the temple block also merits special mention—the wabet ("pure soul") room. This is a covered area for cultic ritual, open on one side to an adjacent, unroofed sun court and near one of the temple's stairs. The room is segregated from the court by two Hathor-headed columns with integrated partial height screen walls, bisected by a shallow stair leading to a broken lintel archway. This was an important space in celebrating "Wepet Renpet" (the Festival of the New Year), where it acted as a secure place to hold the cult figure until it was carried to the roof to await the dawning of Amun-Ra. It was surprising to come across an unroofed courtyard in the center of this massive building, but other late temples, such as the Horus Temple at Edfu, also include this light-filled ritual space.

In addition to the magnificence of the architecture, Dendera has the largest system of crypts in Egypt. To access the underground vault with the "Dendera Light," it is necessary to crawl through a very small opening. That particular crypt space is long but narrow and not tall in section. Marvelous, detailed wall carvings in bas-relief cover all walls and the ceiling, and it is a sobering thought to realize that very few visited this space after completion 1,500 years ago.

From the main level, a very long stepped ramp takes us to the stone paved roof and a higher elevation that provides us with extensive views of Hathor's domain and beyond. In the southwest corner of the roof is a stone chapel, built by the Romans for rituals, especially important for the festival of Wepet Renpet. On that day, the Hathor effigy, by way of the western stair, would make the journey from the sanctuary to the roof temple to bask in the radiance of the rising Amun.

Similar to the Kiosk of Trajan at Philae, only in miniature, the structure, rectangular in plan, is hypaethral, covered at one time with a material awning and now open to the sky. Hathor-headed, cow-eared capitals (also defaced) top the twelve columns at the perimeter, which support a continuous fascia beam above, with screen walls below filling the area between the columns. Two entrances, stone doorframes with broken lintels, interrupt the screen walls. The cult goddess, who in various tales could be the daughter or mother of Amun-Ra, would have been carried to this enclosure to await the appearance of the sun god.

Additional, significant architectural features of note are the very large and prominent water spouts on the sides and rear elevations of the main temple block. Here the spouts take on the sculpted form of a lion's head providing detail and shadow to significant expanses of windowless stone walls, articulated only by shallow carvings. The south façade, a beautifully proportioned expanse of windowless solid stone, battered at each end, is graced by fourteen enormous bas-reliefs sculptures of royalty and gods displayed in a nearly symmetrical arrangement, like a giant billboard or a weighty tome opened to pages of illustration. Among the figures is a rare depiction of Cleopatra VII (the main temple was completed during her reign) and her son, Caesarion, fathered, supposedly, by Julius Caesar.

Dendera's Sacred Lake, located on the west side of the temple, is also architecturally remarkable. At approximately 100 feet by 90 feet, it is large; its walls on all four sides, made of limestone

Interior Wabet Court / Dendera

Rooftop Kiosk / Dendera

View from Temple of Isis / Dendera

blocks, rise above ground level to create a massively wide railing at the perimeter and extend down (approximately fifteen feet) to what would have been the bottom of the lake. At each corner, the rail is interrupted by a stone portal with a broken lintel, presumably to accommodate the height of the deity figure atop its barque when taken to the lake for cult ceremonies.

Each of the four openings features a stair that leads down to the lake; these are architecturally interesting in that they are arranged in a pinwheel orientation around the perimeter, so when descending any of the stairs, visitors are facing the stair on the adjacent wall, perpendicular to their descent. At present a grouping of palm trees populates the derelict lake enclosure, their curving trunks rise from the below grade sandy bottom and burst into a cloud of dark green, spiky leafage, an eerie effect when seen from ground level where the trunks are not visible.

Directly behind the Temple of Hathor is the ruin of the Isis Temple, substantially plundered except for parts of the inner chamber. Column bases and foundations are extant, so it is possible to reconstruct the remainder of this little structure.

The Roman-built mammisi, to the north as we entered, is similar in design and layout as the Mammisi of Edfu—a rectangular block, defined on three sides with an open colonnade and an enclosed courtyard at the entrance. Presently, most of the entrance courtyard has disappeared, but a good deal of the main block remains, although in a reduced state.

At the end of our visit, standing on the stone roof of the temple, we take our final panoramic view of the site and its dark rolling mass of dirt, mud brick and miscellaneous debris, the once resplendent walled precinct of a venerated goddess. We descend and pass through the maze of tall chambers that will take us to the vestibule and out toward the Nile.

Temple of Isis / Dendera

We pause once again to take in the splendid ornament of the pronaos, marveling at the eighteen columns in this spatially rich vestibule, each crowned with a capital of Hathor heads. Column shafts and walls are carved with figures highlighted by ghostly traces of turquoise and ochre, and the entire ethos of this chamber is redolent with the aura of ancient Egypt—the spatial quality, horizontally close and vertically tall, is a masterpiece of architectural design. It is a vessel of enchantment whose spell remained long after stepping across the threshold into the brilliance of the late afternoon sun.

Philae Island

DAY 11

The Goddess Isis:

I *AM AMONG THE MOST REVERED of the ancients, not only by the Egyptians, but by the Greeks and Romans as well. My figure is represented by that of a woman holding a reed in one hand and the ankh in the other, my head adorned with a crown in the form of a throne to represent my close association with the pharaoh. Later in my reign, I took on the association with Hathor and may be depicted with a solar disc mounted between a crown of cow's horns. In addition, I am often rendered with long, feathered wings, spread to provide protection in life as well as in death. Among my domains is first and foremost magic, including healing and vivification of the dead and then the wide realm of nature in its various forms.*

My sensitivity is that of a woman, a wife, and a mother, prompting empathy and protection of the weak and poor, but my infinite powers are often employed in circumstances of a different nature. My influence extended into the 4th century AD and Philae Island was once the center of my veneration.

View of Temple Complex from Nile River / Philae Island

View to Great Court / Philae Island

Kiosk of Nectanebo / Philae Island

LIKE THE ENCHANTED ISLES of Circe and Shakespeare's Prospero ("full of noises, sounds, and sweet airs"), the island of Philae was once a place of magic spells and sorcery. Here, the cult of Isis, goddess of nature and magic, wife of Osiris and mother to Horus, was celebrated in mystery rituals accommodated in an architecture of variety and striking allure that is still, despite flood, desert storms, and relocation, among Egypt's best preserved and most beautiful temple complexes.

A boat takes us along the western edge of the temple complex to the island's southern point. From this moving perspective, sailing parallel to the long axis of the island, we have a panoramic view of Philae's western edge and one of ancient Egypt's most breathtaking sights. A tall stone wall defining the great outer courtyard starts at the southern tip and ends just before the temple façade, allowing for a glimpse of the Gate of Ptolemy II with the Kiosk of Trajan just beyond. Next, the first pylon springs up to create the edge of the majestic temple structure. Bridging the space between the first and second sets of pylons is the mammisi, articulated on the west façade by a row of low screen walls and engaged columns, topped with opulent capitals. In this case, the colonnade lends an element of detail and a depth of shadow, providing visual relief from the solidity and weight of the windowless stone walls of the western façades. Completing the composition is the Temple of Isis, composed of the impressive second set of pylons and the contiguous block of worship and administrative spaces.

Taking in the entire breadth of the island and its structures (at over 600 feet), the abstracted image is that of a grand, stately vessel on this wide river, with its shimmering reflection inverted and fluid, as if seen in another reality. It is an entrancing introduction to the riches of this architectural masterpiece, seemingly afloat on the Nile.

Kiosk of Nectanebo / Philae Island

This island, in truth, is not Philae, but Agilkia. In the 1960s, Philae's monuments, periodically flooded after the construction of the Aswan Dam, were dismantled and relocated to a higher elevation on this nearby island.

Kiosk of Nectanebo / Philae Island

Great Court Colonnade Detail / Philae Island

Architecture / Outer Courtyard

AFTER A STUNNING INTRODUCTION to Philae, as viewed from the Nile, we disembark at the south end of the island. From this vantage, a wide view from east to west encompasses the magnificent superstructure of the Kiosk of Trajan, just above the tree line, with its fourteen luxurious capitals and open column grid; the Isis Temple pylons in the far distance; the great outer courtyard defined by its massive colonnades; and the Kiosk of Nectanebo, with its single, miniature obelisk adding a vertical flourish near the water's edge.

The great court, directly before us, partially defined by the first set of pylons, is spatially dynamic; it is enclosed by two long colonnades of massive columns, oblique in relation to each other, which establish a formal cadence of movement as the court splays out to the temple entrance. A solid stone wall behind each row of columns defines the extent and shape of the space. On the Nile side of the east wall are contiguous structures: the remains of the Chapel of Mandulis and the Temple of Imhotep (the architect of Djoser's Step Pyramid at Saqqara), both significantly reduced in material.

Nectanebo's Kiosk, with its expressed column structure, anchors the southern point of the island, appearing to have broken free of the west colonnade and sharply tilted east, directing movement and perspective out into the Nile and its host of small, adjacent islands.

The Temple of Isis is the most prominent structure here, beautiful in its cubical and tapered masses and distinctive with its two sets of twin pylon towers. Each pylon of the first set is animated with billboard-size bas-reliefs of gods and royalty; among the deities, Hathor, Isis, and Horus are in attendance while Pharaoh Ptolemy XII Neos Dionysus is illustrated smiting his enemy and triumphant in battle. It is like a single frame of action from a constantly moving depiction of history, a mixture of religious and civic propaganda, writ large.

From the courtyard, we move up to the elevation of the entrance gate by way of a stepped ramp positioned between two granite lion statues flanking the ornately embellished portal, which is topped by the ubiquitous cavetto molding and embellished with the typical winged sun motif. To the right, directly before the entrance opening is the Gate of Ptolemy II, a freestanding stone portal with an east/west orientation, also capped with the cavetto molding. Through its open passageway, we see the Kiosk of Trajan in the near distance.

Collectively, this ensemble of colonnades, kiosks, heroically scaled pylons, freestanding stone gate portal, masterful carvings, and evocative iconography yields a rich architectural experience that once served as an appropriately scaled, monumental backdrop to ceremony and spectacle. Despite the span of building over hundreds of years and numerous dynasties, the monuments at Philae, like other ancient sites, establish a stylistic sympathy across time, united in material and ornament and purpose.

View West from Trajan's Kiosk / Philae Island

Gate of Ptolemy II + Trajan's Kiosk / Philae Island

Gate of Ptolemy II / Philae Island

Inner Courtyard / Mammisi

FROM THE OUTER COURTYARD, we move through the first set of pylons into the inner courtyard, a space defined by an open colonnade (ten elegantly proportioned columns topped with a variety of capital designs) to the right, the mammisi to the left, and the second set of pylons directly ahead.

I found the mammisi to hold the greatest interest and the greatest inspiration: It is a masterly balance of mass, decoration, and proportion. The atypical location, spanning between two sets of pylons, means the long façade becomes a major edge in defining the courtyard space and a visual enrichment with its luxurious sculpted decoration. Typically, the mammisi is located before a temple entrance, set perpendicular to axial movement to the sanctuary (as at Edfu or Dendera). Here, the long façade of the mammisi is integrated into the Isis Temple plan (the entrance door aligns with a passage through the first west pylon) to great artistic effect, with its columns acknowledging those to the east, while a matching colonnade on the west elevation adds a visually exciting façade toward the Nile, creating a "hyphen" between pylons. The whole is a kind of "decorated box" where the original structure of two chambers was enlarged by a third and then circumscribed by a superstructure of fascia and a narrow colonnade on three sides. The addition of screen walls between columns creates the sensation of a "building within a building," and the small mammisi entry porch, which faces the back of the first set of pylons, is adorned with two engaged and two freestanding columns, making for a beautifully scaled portico.

A subtle, but significant architectural experience occurs between the mammisi entry façade and the rear elevation of the first pylon, a space only six feet wide at the pavement level, where both façades angle upward. Here is a small spatial transition that is a magical interval of architectural design. In moving through this narrow space, from the inner courtyard to the river side of the

Mammisi + Temple Forecourt / Philae Island

Mammisi Entrance Detail / Philae Island

mammisi, there is a feeling of compression as one is "squeezed" through its short length (depending on the number of tourists), creating a palpable engagement with the architecture and intensifying the feeling of release at facing the wide expanse of the Nile upon exiting. Architecturally, it is a modest yet powerful experience.

Temple of Isis

CONTINUING WITH A SLIGHT ANGLE SHIFT in our path, we are now on axis with the sanctuary, facing the full façade of the second set of pylons. At a height of forty feet, they are shorter than the first set of pylons, but similar in their depiction of the pharaoh making offerings to the gods. The formal portal gate between the pylons is squared off at the top: Either the moldings and cavetto curve at the parapet were destroyed or the gate was never completed. This façade has also suffered damage to the sculpted images.

In the northeast corner of the courtyard, contiguous with the eastern colonnade, are the foundation ruins of a small Christian church. Directly behind it is an impressively large granite stela in the shape of a rounded slab mounted vertically and integrated into the base of the eastern pylon, depicting Ptolemy VI Philometor and Cleopatra II with Isis and Horus. There is another shallow step-ramp up to the temple entrance (similar to the first pylon approach), and we enter into the relatively modest hypostyle hall, a space adorned and supported by ten columns arranged in a "U" configuration. The space, however, is transformed with an atrium-like opening above, adjacent to the pylon, filling in the center of the "U." This surprising feature allows natural light to fill the space, molding the columns in shadow and giving the visitor a view of the sky and the rear face of the tower above. This small "vessel of light" is in contrast to the windowless darkness of the remainder of the spaces.

We then move into the body of the temple through three simply laid out antechambers, stepping over the threshold of the central space into the Sanctuary of Isis, which is still equipped with the pedestal used to support the sacred barque.

All the elements of pomp, pageantry, and heroic architecture in an ancient processional ritual would have been merely a prelude to arrival in this relatively tiny space where the physical effigy embodying the spirit of the goddess Isis resided in ancient times.

Kiosk of Trajan

AS THE MOST PROMINENT STRUCTURE on the eastern side of the island, the imposing Kiosk of Trajan sits on a stone podium that juts out toward the Nile, establishing its prominence in the foreground with smaller structures placed in what appear to be random locations along this stretch of the river's edge, extending north.

With its exceptionally striking structure of fourteen expressed columns and their luxuriant, foliated capitals, Trajan's Kiosk is among the most beautiful structures of ancient Egypt to have survived the vicissitudes of time, river immersion, and desert climate. Positioned in close proximity to the water's edge on the eastern side of the island, it served as a stopping place during the transportation of the cult effigy of Isis on its journey to the temple sanctuary. Its purpose was a pure conception of the imagination catalyzed by a leap of faith: It defined a spiritually protected haven with the graven image of the deity, safe within its magical boundary, the imagined forces of chaos checked around its perimeter.

Once roofed, its perimeter grid of columns and beams set against blue sky create a unique structure whose spatial definition is both open and closed. The lower half of the kiosk is composed of typical screen walls that engage the columns. This relationship, seen on our travels in numerous structures from temples to kiosks

Mammisi + Entry Pylons / Philae Island

Trajan's Kiosk / Philae Island

Kiosk Columns + Fascia / Philae Island

Temple of Isis Façade: 2nd Pylons / Philae Island

to mammisi, is a slight overlapping of the screen wall with the round column, creating a perceived "bulge" effect where the curve of the support appears to be compressed by the wall. Thus, the structure is integrated and complete, but still allows a reading of the parts as base, wall, column, impost, and fascia.

Additional Structures

Smaller and less preserved than the Kiosk of Trajan, the Kiosk of Nectanebo now consists of only the foundation, four nearly complete columns, wall remnants, and part of the fascia superstructure. Still, it adds a dynamic insertion into the layout of the outer courtyard, tilted away from the end of the western colonnade to direct movement and a view inflected to the south. One of the two small obelisks once marking the edge of the enclosure still exists and it adds a vertical element, taking the eye from pylon to colonnade to river.

The eastern side of the island, in contrast to our approach view, is less dense with structures and softened with a greater amount of vegetation. Complementing the larger structures and massive colonnades on Philae are a number of smaller temples and gates, all somewhat plundered and/or reduced: Two small temples to Arensnuphis and Imhotep and the Chapel of Mandulis (a Nubian sun god) are contiguous to the outer courtyard's eastern wall.

Then moving north from Trajan's Kiosk, the remains of temples to Hathor and Augustus seem randomly placed near the edge of the riverbank, with each pivoted off the orthogonal to face the

Temple of Isis Interior Vestibule / Philae Island

Nile, while quay and temple remnants, thought to be built by the Roman Emperor Diocletian, are positioned at the northeast projection of the island, oriented to the north.

Considered in its entirety, Philae is among the richest of architectural ruins that has survived from ancient times—the quality of its execution and the spatial variety represent a virtually unrivaled wealth of artistic excellence.

At the conclusion of our visit, we ride along the eastern edge of Philae Island on our return to Aswan and experience another perspective of what must have been, with its distinctive siting, an astonishing presence in antiquity. Where Egypt's other temples established a massive, static presence rising from the Sahara, the majestic Isis Temple complex appears in motion on the Nile, the perennial life force of this land. In this magical realm, the goddess of nature took up her residence, and the generous breadth of the great formal entry courtyard with its ample columns and ornate capitals, the dignified grandeur of the temple, the stately presence of Trajan's Kiosk, and the delicate beauty of its mammisi attest to the significance of the Isis cult and the devotion of her followers.

Mammisi Detail / Philae Island

Hathor Temple / Philae Island

Hathor Temple / Philae Island

Hieroglyph

Hathor Temple / Philae Island

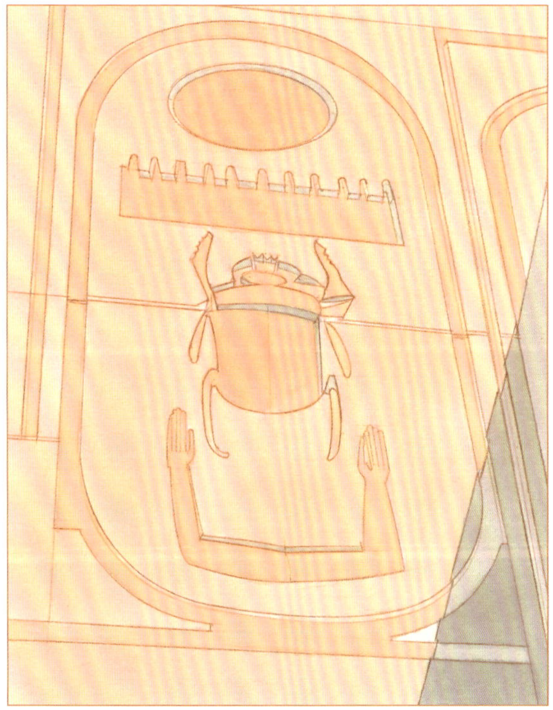

Hieroglyph: Sacred Scarab

View from Nile River / Philae Island

Temple of Ramesses II

IMAGE ONE

22 February 1220 BC

AS THE REBORN GOD AMUN-RA emerges from his hazardous journey through the Duat, the underworld realm of the dead, his radiance consumes the night, gradually illuminating the domed kingdom of the night goddess Nut.

During the ascent, the great fiery eye of Amun casts a direct beam through the entry door centered between flanking figures of Ramesses II at the massive rock temple at Abu Simbel. Piercing the darkness, the ray illuminates three of the four statues of seated gods sculpted on the rear wall in the last space of the temple, a distance of over 160 feet from the entrance.

The figures are the dedicatees of this shrine: Amun-Ra, Ra-Horakhty, the deified Ramesses II, and Ptah of Memphis, a shadowed figure not directly illuminated by the sun deity.

It is the birthday of King Ramesses II "the Great." This radiating benediction will occur again on 22 October 1220 BC, and thereafter twice a year for eternity, animating this vessel cut from living rock in reverence to Amun.

Symbolizing the solar cult and standing in permanence above the entry is the sculpted figure of Ra-Horakhty, strikingly crowned with a great solar disc as he takes a shallow step forward from the rock face as Egypt's avatar of the sun at its zenith.

Ramesses II Detail / Abu Simbel

IMAGE TWO

01 May 1969 AD

AMONG THE MORE STRIKING IMAGES of the 1960s are the photographs of the center section of Ramesses II's head being lifted by crane to its new position 200 feet above the original location of the sculpted figure, once shaped in situ from the shear vertical face of mountain rock at Abu Simbel.

To avoid total immersion in the waters of the Nile due to the creation of the man-made Lake Nasser, the temples of both Ramesses II and Nefertari (first of the Great Royal Wives) were cut into blocks, reassembled and integrated into a new concrete structure designed to resemble the original mountain form. Only the hairline joints of the various reassembled pieces hint at the mammoth relocation effort. The undertaking of moving two entire mountain faces and their associated interior chambers (also excavated from the mountain rock) represents one of the greatest engineering feats of 20th-century technology, although, as some may say, equally matched by the bold vision of the original undertaking at this remote, outer edge of an empire, 3,300 years ago.

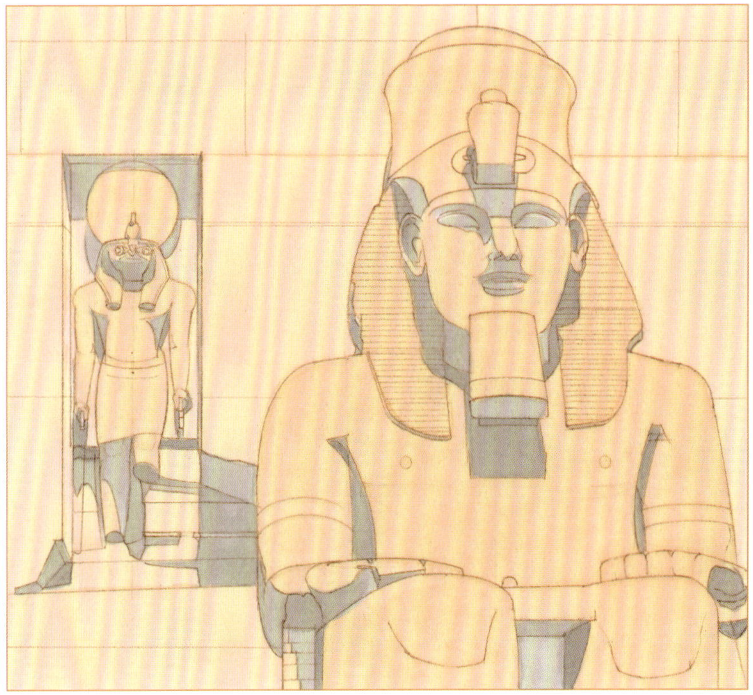

Ra-Horakhty + Ramesses II / Abu Simbel

Abu Simbel

DAY 12

IN EARLY MORNING, we flew over miles of vacant desert to arrive at Abu Simbel before the enveloping heat of midday. Once we arrive at the site, we move toward the back of the hulking mass of the man-made mountain of concrete that now accommodates the temple façades on the lake side, facing away from our approach.

As we move along the edge of the mound, the panorama widens, taking in the lake and the horizon; continuing in our arc, the Temple of Nefertari appears first in the distance; we then round the corner and the four titanic Ramesses figures and the temple façade fill the entire foreground. Seeing the Ramesses Temple slowly appear as we make our way around the mountain is a thrilling experience, at once strange and overwhelming. Its majesty dominates a landscape that has no context aside from the vertical face of the mountain, the shimmering horizontal plane of water and the thin line of a distant horizon. The vivid, painted colors on the quartet of pharaohs, gods, and apotropaic cultic animals and hieroglyphics that once covered the figures have faded with time and sun, leaving the whole to return to the ubiquitous color of primeval desert.

Now at the end of our journey, we stand on a narrow swath of excoriated desert between the four colossi of Ramesses II and the man-made Lake Nasser. Standing spellbound before the pharaoh's temple, nearly 600 miles south of Cairo, we have reached the outermost rim of our travels; the Sudan and remote Africa lie beyond to the south.

Time and normative physical reference have little meaning here. The feeling of isolation is manifest; it is the biblical sense of being a stranger in a strange land, exiled to a remote planet or frontier outpost, standing before what might be life-size images of an alien king or deity. Upon its completion in the 13th century BC,

Ramesses II Statues at Entry Vestibule / Abu Simbel

Temple Façade / Abu Simbel

one can imagine the sense of terror inspired by not just a single Ramesses, but a quartet of brightly rendered colossi towering above the shore, then doubled, as reflected in the trembling waters of the Nile. If there was any doubt of allegiance, this remote temple established the imperium of an omnipotent desert king with the power to smite his enemies from hundreds of miles away.

This was to be the final construction by Ramesses II in Nubia.

Architecture

THERE ARE ACTUALLY TWO ROCK CUT TEMPLES at Abu Simbel—the larger for Pharaoh Ramesses II and the smaller for his favorite queen, Nefertari, both sculpted in situ, shaped from living stone and separated by a distance of 300 feet. In both, niches frame the figures: one large recess for the four Ramesses figures and six individual recesses, one for each statue at the Queen Nefertari Temple. Each is visible from the other's location.

The Ramesses Temple is a brilliant display of the social and religious standing of the pharaoh; he has reigned here in silent authority as a symbol of Egyptian power and an intimidating presence for 3,000 years, once arousing fear in neighboring states and today inspiring wonder (and possibly some fear) in visitors.

Temple of Ramesses the Great

AT EGYPTIAN TEMPLES (Luxor, for example), statues of the pharaoh flanking the entrance portal gate are relatively small in scale and supplemental to the overall façade. Here, the four statues of the seated Ramesses II, each at a height of sixty-five feet, dominate the entire breadth of this rock-cut temple with two seated statues on either side of the small entrance to the interior. Numerous smaller figures of the king's family are sculpted around the legs of each of the four Ramesses effigies.

Positioned directly above the single-door entrance in a recessed niche is the falcon-headed, human-shaped statue of Ra-Horakhty, his head adorned with the cobra Uraeus and a massive sun disc. In contrast to the static figures of the flanking pair of Ramesses, the god is captured in mid-stride, appearing to emerge from the rock face.

As a backdrop, the façade rises behind the figures with sloped wall edges meant to approximate the shape of a freestanding temple pylon; its crowning frieze is adorned with 22 baboons in heliolatry pose, heads tilted and arms out acknowledging the sun. At ground level, a plinth with numerous small figures of Horus and the pharaoh marks the edge of the temple entity, and a shallow stone ramp joins the desert floor to the entry plinth and the doorway to the temple interior.

The temple façade is nearly symmetrical with the visitor entering on axis between the flanking statues, two on each side (the head and part of the upper torso of one Ramesses statue lies before it on the sand, the result of an earthquake in 27 BC).

The ancients, always bent on impressing with height and magnitude, created an entry hall strikingly defined with two rows of four Ramesses statues, thirty feet in height and facing one another, which divide the entry into three distinct chambers.

In typical fashion, the walls and ceilings are covered with numerous painted designs and scenes of the pharaoh and his wife, with

Temple of Nefertari Façade: Detail / Abu Simbel

Temple of Nefertari Hathor Capital Detail / Abu Simbel

the most impressive images being those of Ramesses in battle. The supposed victory against the Hittites at the Battle of Kadesh, with Ramesses delivering blows to his enemy, is conspicuously featured in various tableau of great artistic beauty and refinement.

At the rear of the temple are the four rock-cut figures seated next to each other facing the entrance, awaiting the direct brilliance of the sun and its illumination twice a year.

Temple of Nefertari

THE TEMPLE OF NEFERTARI (the smaller temple), located 300 feet east of the great Ramesses figures, was also cut in situ. Modest in comparison to the pharaoh's temple, yet still impressive in height (fifty feet) and breadth (100 feet), the nearly symmetrical façade is graced by six standing figures, each thirty feet tall. Four sculptures are of Pharaoh Ramesses II and two sculptures are of Nefertari (deified as Isis-Hathor), with the queen figure standing as tall as that of the king, a rare acknowledgment in this culture. Each figure and its niche are sculpted from the mountain face, which creates a sloping "buttress-like" effect on the remaining rock profile between statues. In this case, the level of workmanship in the sculpting is less refined than that of the Great Sphinx, for example—another monolithic rock sculpture worked in place. This may be a result of the quality of artisans working in such a remote part of the kingdom or the particular consistency of the stone, but while it lacks subtlety, the façade is still a work of substance, and the giant figures are impressively commanding.

Unlike Ramesses, who sits enthroned and seemingly motionless, the figures at the Nefertari temple are depicted with one leg before the other, emerging from the mountain, a dynamic device to engage the viewer. In the approximate center of the façade is an entrance into a temple appropriately dedicated to the goddess Hathor as well as to Queen Nefertari. The visitor enters on axis

Temple Porch / Abu Simbel

Ramesses Temple + Temple of Nefertari / Abu Simbel

into a small hypostyle hall. Two rows of three Hathor-headed piers (her hair stylishly "flipped" at the ends) opposite one another define the approach to the sanctuary, and numerous depictions of Nefertari and Hathor adorn the walls. The temple is an intimate counterpart to the heroic grandeur of the Ramesses Temple, a few hundred feet away.

The ageless gods of ancient Egypt inhabited the media of earth, water, fire, and air, consecrating the elements with their immortal and sacred natures. In distinct contrast to the quarried and assembled stones of the pyramids and temples, Abu Simbel's living rock held the divinity of the pharaoh and his queen within the dimension of the earth gods and goddesses who resided therein.

To reveal this power and divinity only required the release of the figures from this remote cliff in the form of sculpted, three-dimensional representations of their true, sacred selves, while the hollowed mountains held the body of each temple in perfect, eternal equilibrium.

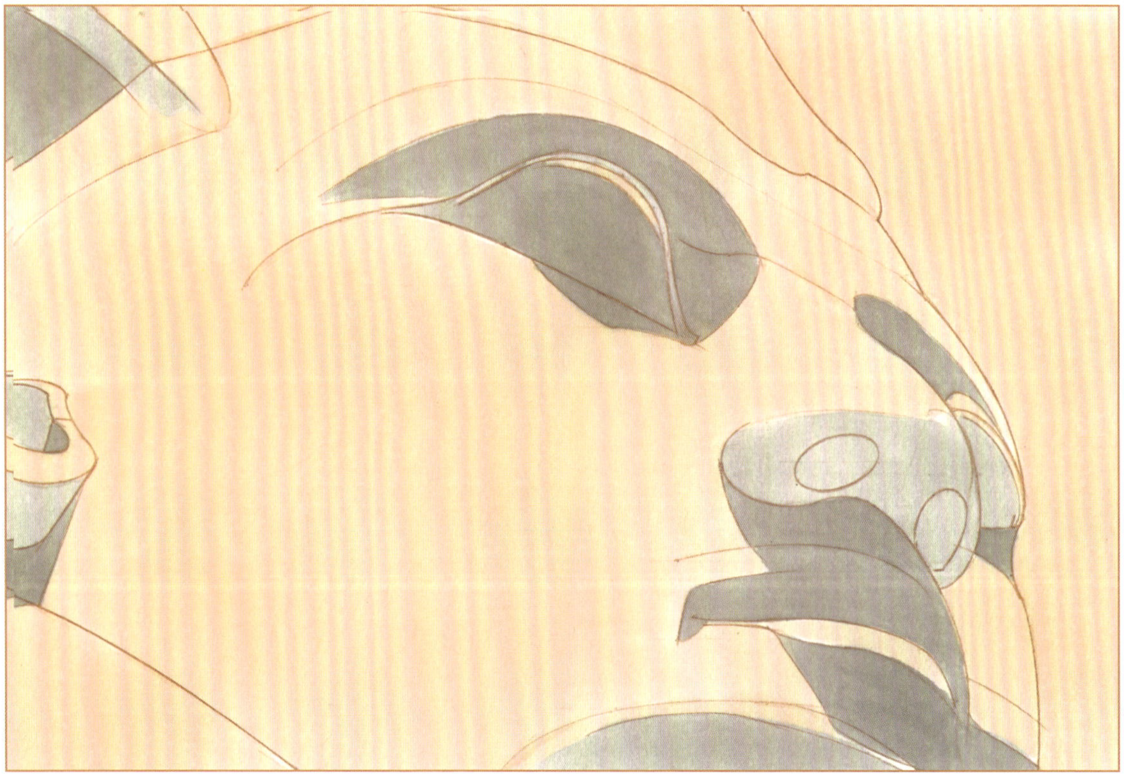

Ramesses II Detail / Abu Simbel

Art + Architecture: II

POSTSCRIPT

FLYING OUT OF CAIRO'S International Airport, the earth drops away into one vast expanse of Saharan sand and rock for as far as the eye can see; it is a landscape distinguished only by subtle variations of beige, tinged with yellow, riven by the Nile and its swath of dark alluvial green. The Giza Pyramids are only discernible as three elongated, chevron-pointed shadows of different lengths, and, in the distance, the city is a variegated, brownish hodgepodge of boxy, irregular shapes. These are the colors of desert life, both ancient and modern, past and future.

There was a time when only Amun-Ra surveyed the lands of this domain from this height. As we ascend, the massive constructions of temple and pyramid are like pieces in a board game, small tokens of similitude. Then, all the grandeur and fantasy are flattened into homogeneity and blended into the terrain.

On the ground, however, standing transfixed before the architecture, we felt the presence of those who came before us, fashioned remarkable and sublime works of art from raw nature, and left a wide array of stunning artifacts whose aesthetic perfection may still overwhelm the senses. The architecture was once again alive while we were under its spell, each sign and symbol had something to reveal about these ancient people.

As we walked among the ruins, the creators of these mysteries, now suspended in distant time, stepped out of the shadows for a moment to help us understand the ancient will and the cultural force that envisioned and built these wonders in a desolate desert setting.

Today and every day, a new wave of travelers courses through these massive temple halls or descends into subterranean chambers or surveys the banks of the Nile on a languorous cruise upriver. Khufu's Pyramid will undoubtedly stand for all time, continuing into a future state that has no vanishing point as defined by man; the soul of the Egyptian, once reanimated by the magical ankh to the lips, has also found perpetuity across the threshold of death into eternity, entering a cosmic dimension once and forever sustained by a belief in the ancient gods who still haunt this land.

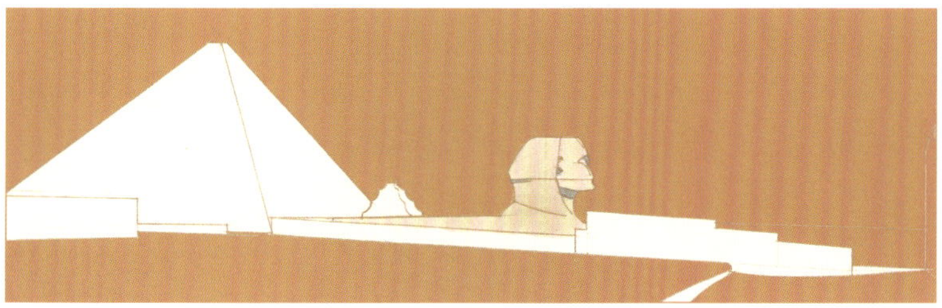

Egypt

IMAGES:

Sacred + Profane

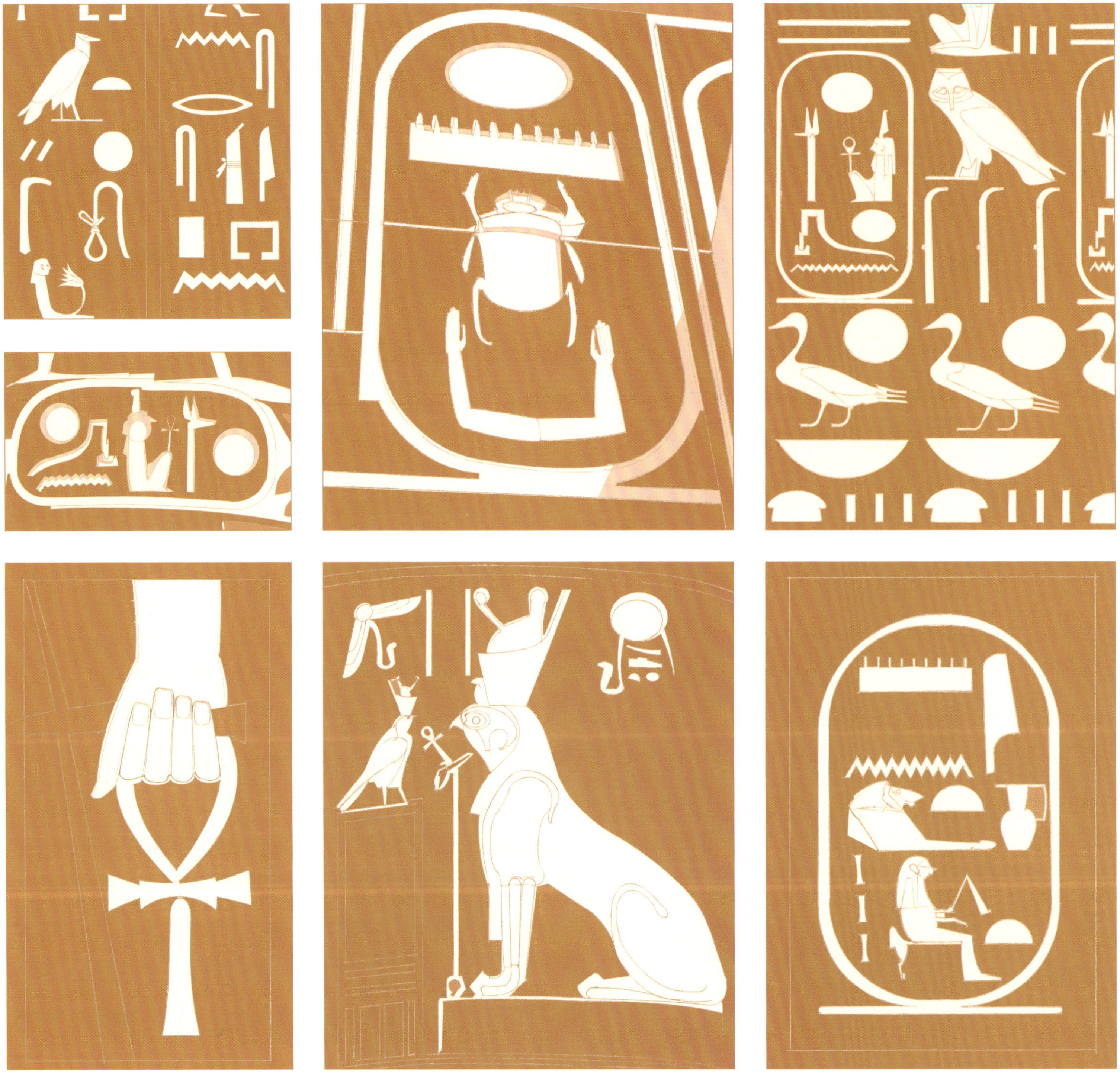

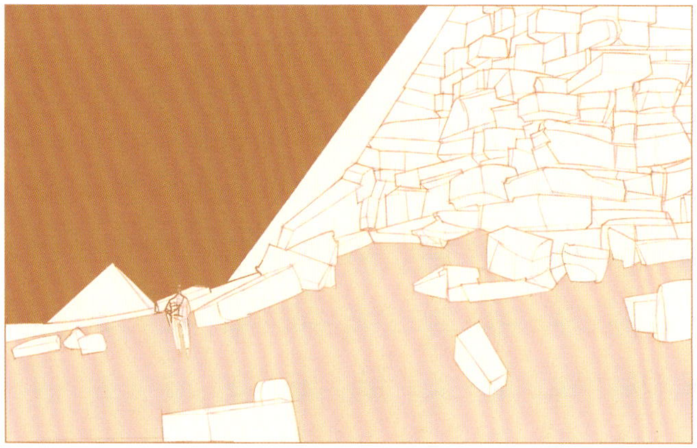

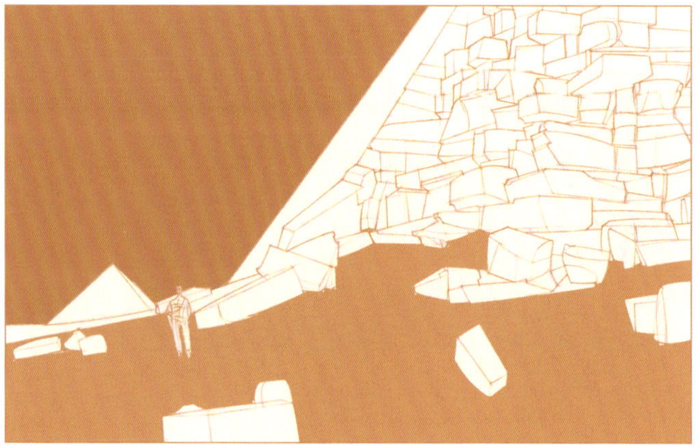

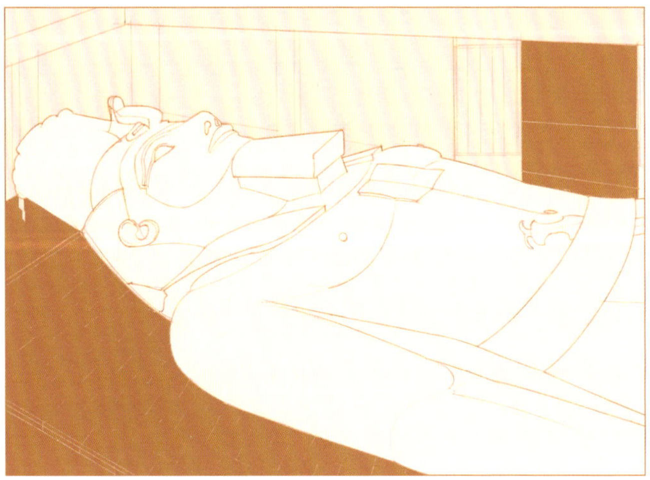

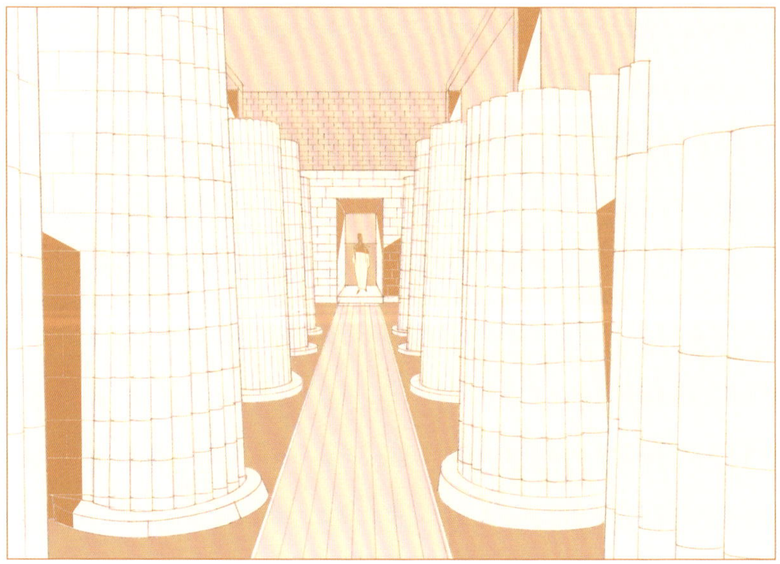

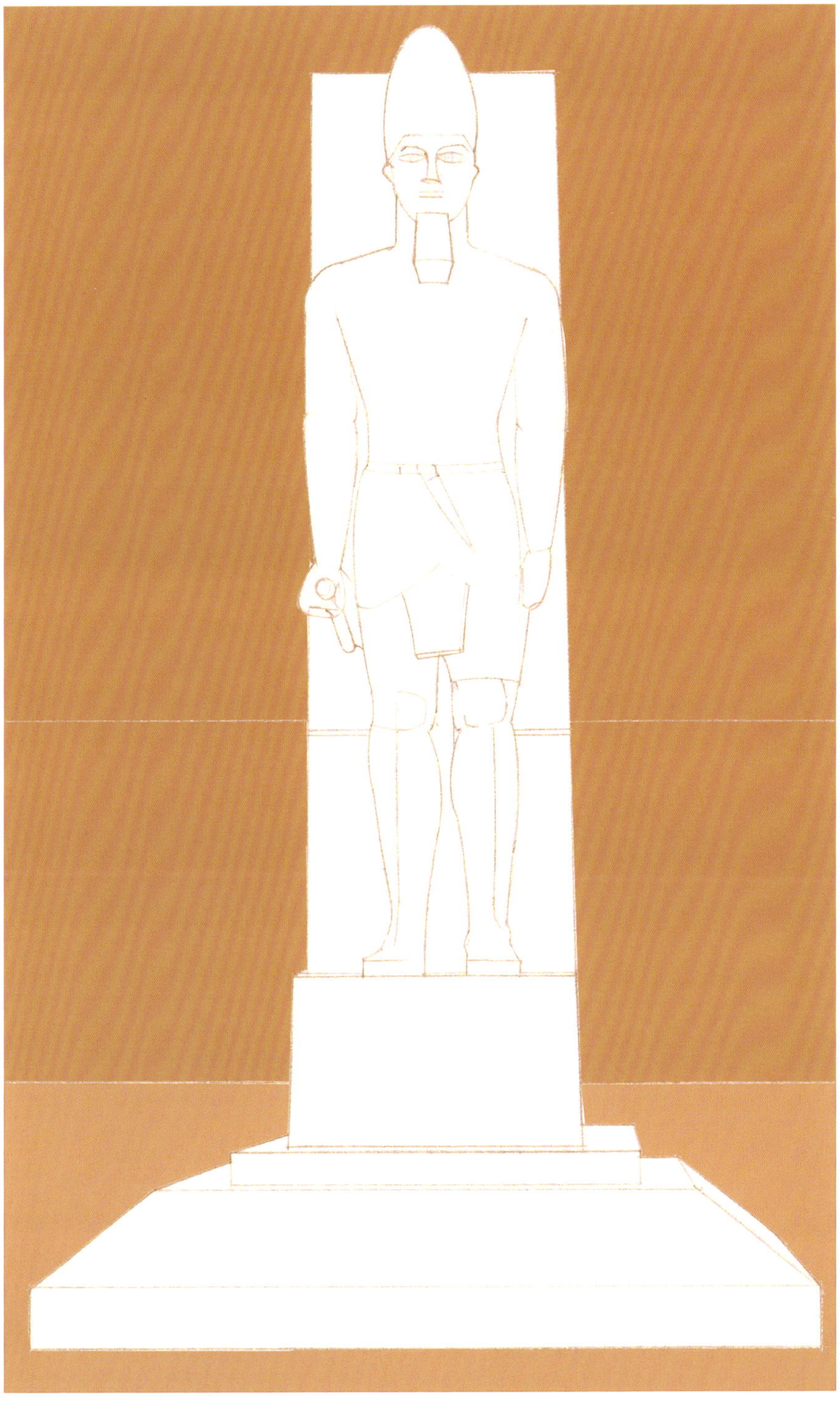

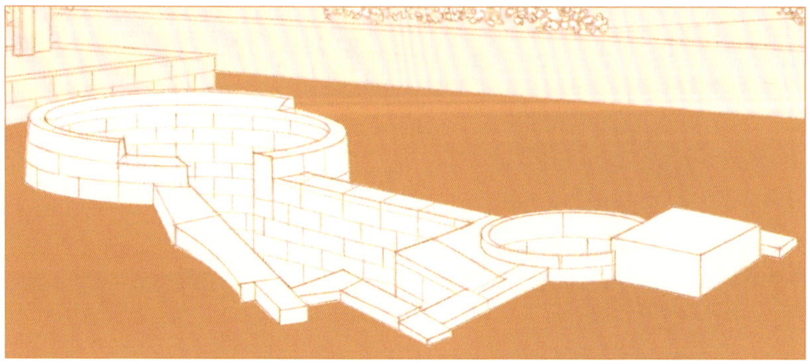

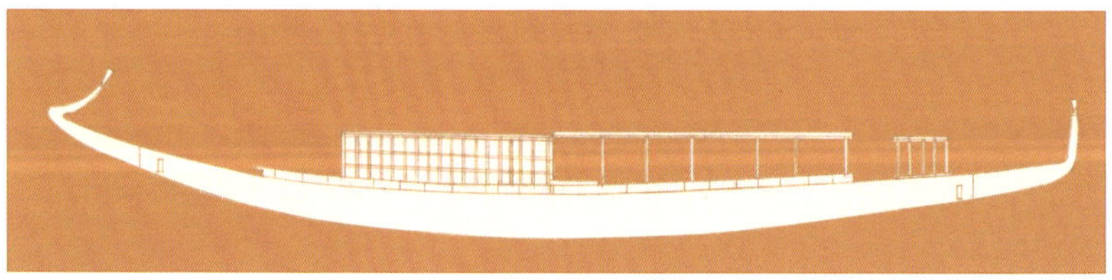

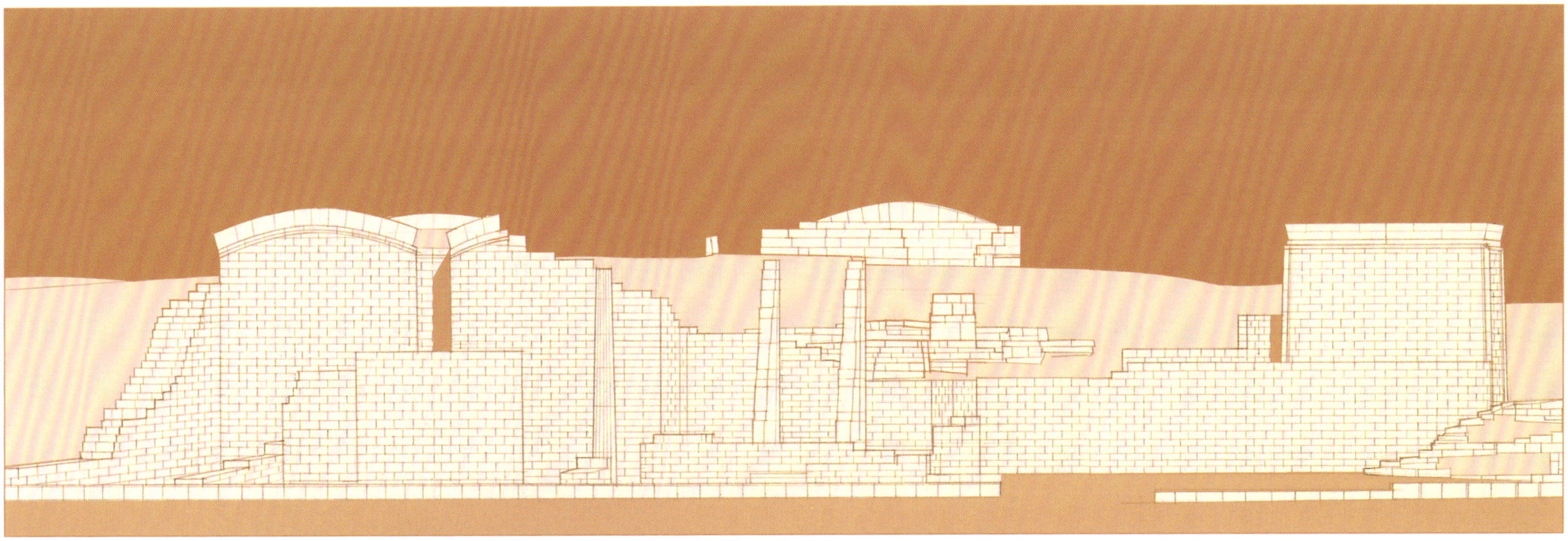

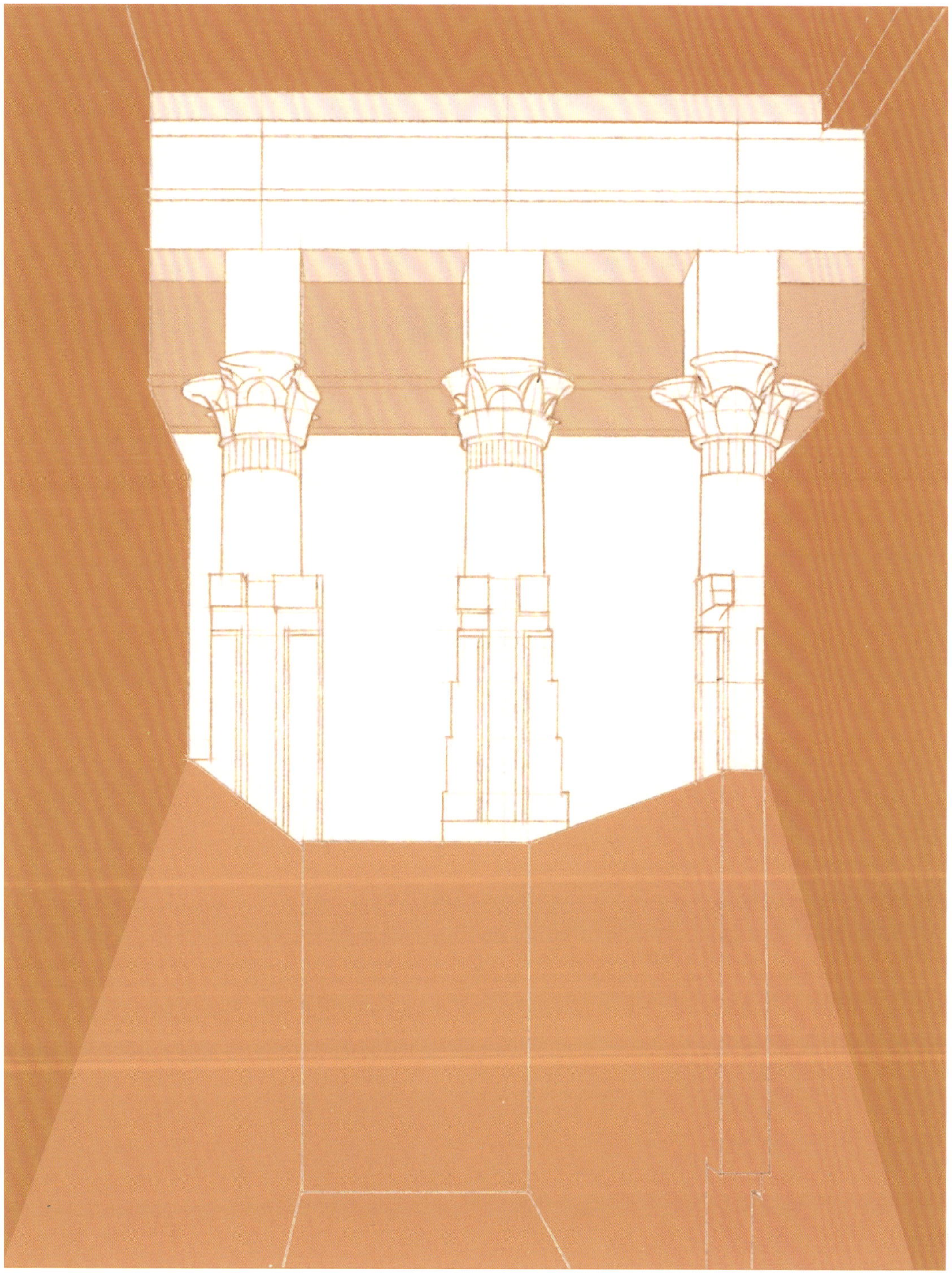

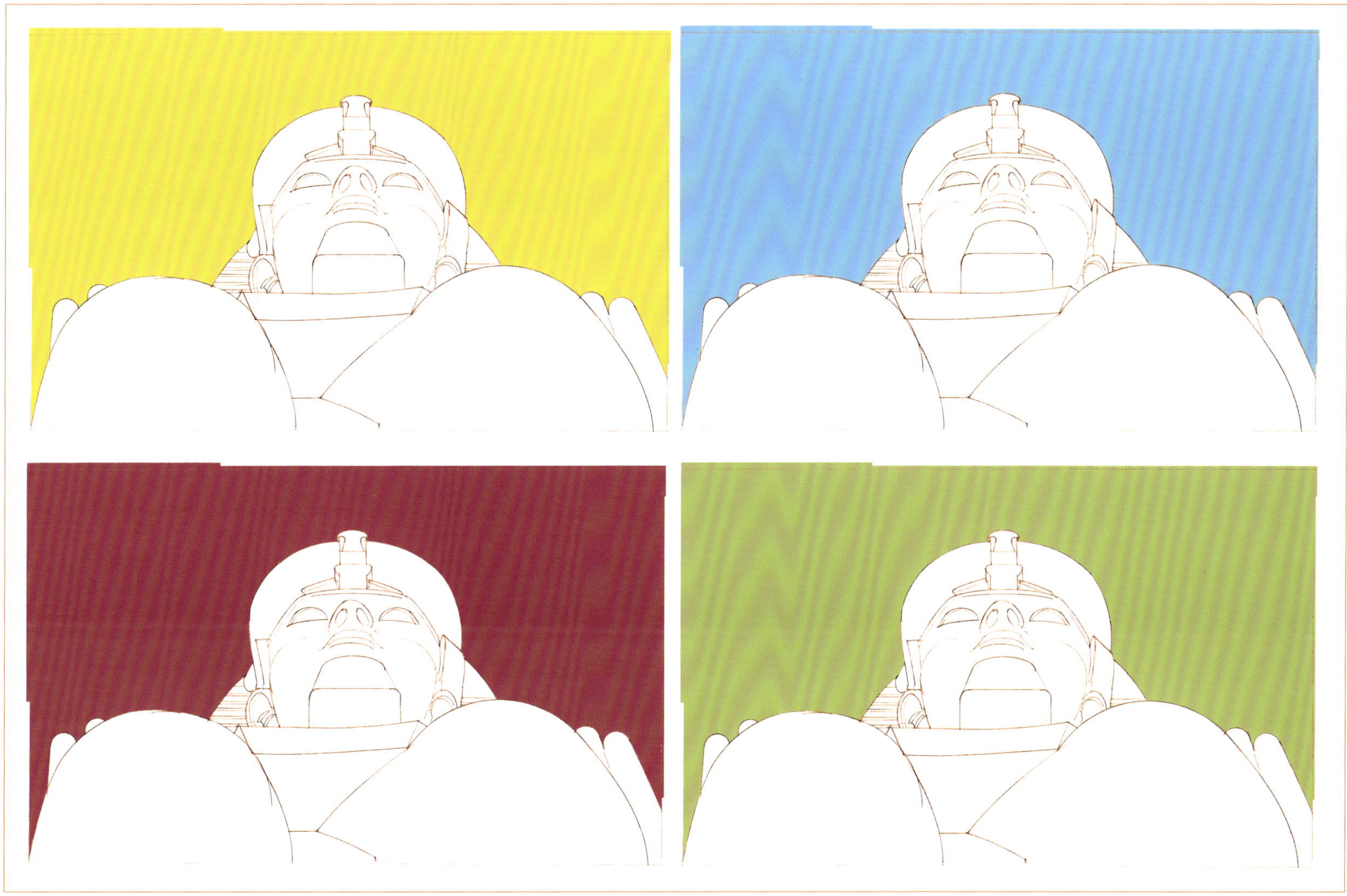

RAMESSES II

Selected Bibliography

Arnold, Dieter. *The Encyclopedia of Ancient Egyptian Architecture*. New York: Princeton University Press, 2003.

Arnold, Dieter. *Temples of the Last Pharaohs*. New York: Oxford University Press, 1999.

Burgess, Anthony. *Homage to QWERT YUIOP and Other Writings*. New York: McGraw Hill Book Company, 1986.

Connolly, Cyril. *The Selected Essays of Cyril Connolly*, edited by Peter Quennell. New York: Persea Books Inc., 1984.

Durand, Françoise and Christiane Zivie-Coche. *Gods and Men in Egypt 3000 BCE to 395 CE*. Ithaca: Cornell University Press, 2004.

Kostof, Spiro. *The Architect*. New York: Oxford University Press, 1977.

LeCorbusier. *Towards a New Architecture*, translated by Frederick Etchells. London: J. Rodker, 1931.

Phillips, J. Peter. *The Columns of Egypt*. Manchester: Peartree Publishing, 2002.

Pinch, Geraldine. *Egyptian Myth*. Oxford: Oxford University Press, 2004.

N. Rambova, ed. *The Shrines of Tut-Ankh-Amun*. New York: Princeton University Press, 1955.

Riggs, Christina. *Ancient Egypt Art and Architecture*. Oxford: Oxford University Press, 2014.

Roehrig, Catharine H., ed., with Renée Dreyfus and Cathleen A. Keller. T*he Career of Senenmut*. New York: The Metropolitan Museum of Art, 2005.

Scully, Vincent Joseph. Architecture: *The Natural and the Manmade*. New York: St. Martin's Press, 1991.

Schwaller de Lubicz, René Adolph. *The Temple in Man: The Secrets of Ancient Egypt*, translated by Robert and Deborah Lawlor. Brookline: Autumn Press, 1977.

Shafer Byron E., ed. *Temples of Ancient Egypt*. Ithaca: Cornell University Press, 1997.

Soane, Sir John. *The Royal Academy Lectures, Lecture I*. Cambridge: Cambridge University Press, 2000.

Media: Koh-i-noor pencil " Progresso" Woodless Color Pencil #8750/11 / Strathmore paper / Chartpak Markers / Adobe Photoshop 2020

ORO EDITIONS

Publishers of Architecture, Art, and Design
Gordon Goff: Publisher

www.oroeditions.com
info@oroeditions.com

Published by ORO Editions

Book Design: Henry David Ayon
Book Layout: Rita Sowins / Sowins Design
Text: Henry David Ayon
ORO Project Coordinator: Kirby Anderson

10 9 8 7 6 5 4 3 2 1 First Edition

Library of Congress data available upon request. World Rights: Available

ISBN: 978-1-951541-21-7

Color Separations and Printing: ORO Group Ltd.
Printed in China.

International Distribution: www.oroeditions.com/distribution

ORO Editions makes a continuous effort to minimize the overall carbon footprint of its publications. As part of this goal, ORO Editions, in association with Global ReLeaf, arranges to plant trees to replace those used in the manufacturing of the paper produced for its books. Global ReLeaf is an international campaign run by American Forests, one of the world's oldest nonprofit conservation organizations. Global ReLeaf is American Forests' education and action program that helps individuals, organizations, agencies, and corporations improve the local and global environment by planting and caring for trees.